Gardening on a Shoestring

...en McKerral is an author and freelance jour-
...st who writes fiction for young people and
...-fiction for gardeners. She has worked in the
...ery industry since 1985, and has had numerous articles and
...tographs published in national and regional magazines and
...spapers. In 1991 she became the South Australian columnist
...*Your Garden* magazine. Helen holds a Diploma of Applied
...nce in Natural Resources and a Graduate Diploma in
...ronmental Studies. She lives in the Adelaide Hills with her
...ner and children.

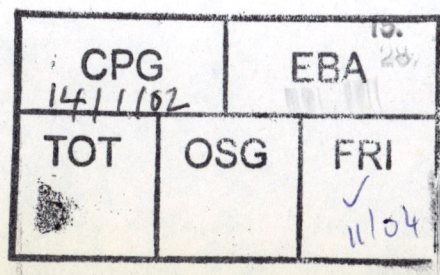

Gardening on a Shoestring

HELEN MCKERRAL

HYLAND HOUSE

First published in Australia in 1999 by
Hyland House Publishing Pty Ltd
Hyland House
387–389 Clarendon Street
South Melbourne
Victoria 3205

National Library of Australia
Cataloguing-in-publication data:

McKerral, Helen.
    Gardening on a shoestring.

    ISBN 1 86447 067 4.

    1. Gardening. I. Title.
635

Design by Rob Cowpe Design
Printed in Australia by Australian Print Group

Contents

Plants to Get You Started

Acknowledgements

I'd like to thank Peter Cookson and Tony O'Brien for their invaluable advice, Annette McFarlane for being my tropical reader, and Celia Cookson for her ideas and for donating so much stuff from her plant nursery. Thanks to Crafers Garden Centre and the Independent Living Centre for letting me photograph their goods, and to my family, Geoff, Dayna and Jody, for their help with the photos.

And finally, thanks to Rose Kitching for being such a thorough (and thoroughly tactful!) editor.

Introduction

This book aims to help you save money—without sacrificing your garden or your enjoyment of gardening. Whether you're new to gardening or more experienced, live in rental accommodation or own a home, this book can help you cut costs and stretch pennies.

You'll find plenty of gardening books in libraries and bookshops, covering every topic from plant propagation to garden design. Many are lavishly illustrated; others are step-by-step guides; others again comprise dense academic or semi-academic texts. All have a place, and if you're keen you've probably already read lots of them. But I've noticed that no matter how inspiring they are, nearly all (big glossy publications especially) assume readers have a limitless budget at their disposal. Money is simply not an issue.

When my partner and I first moved into our new house—sited, seemingly, on a bombsite of clay and rubble—establishing a garden ranked high on our list of priorities. Water pooled in the backyard, and we tramped mud into the house because we had no paths, drains or groundcover plants.

What we *did* have was a two-week-old baby and a large mortgage.

It seems to me ironic that those gardeners most urgently in need of, or most enthusiastic about, establishing and developing a garden are often those with the least disposable income. Like my partner and I once were, many are young couples in new homes, with a substantial proportion of their income committed to paying off the mortgage or providing for young children.

Retired or unemployed gardeners may have more time to spend in their gardens than do working couples with young children but, once again, money is all too often the limiting factor.

If you're a gardener in rental accommodation you have different constraints, because spending big bucks on someone else's garden makes poor financial sense. And yet, why should you deny yourself the pleasure of beautiful and practical surroundings? Why shouldn't you establish a vegetable garden, which can also save you money? How can you beautify the landlady's garden without paying her unnecessary dollars for the privilege?

We're all beginner gardeners at some stage, and it's at this time that it's horribly easy to waste money. How do you recognise bargains? Where do you find them? What's good value for money? What's false economy? What alternatives are available?

Gardeners who own very large gardens don't necessarily own correspondingly large bank accounts. Acreages are expensive to maintain and develop—you need many, many times the numbers of plants to green a hectare than to green a suburban block. And if you're dealing in larger numbers of plants or amounts of pesticide and fertiliser, a single mistake can cost you a lot more money.

If you're a beginning gardener with little or no experience, this book will help you make purchases and planning decisions you won't regret later. *Gardening on a Shoestring* provides practical money-saving techniques. Plant propagation, soil improvement methods and sensible irrigation practices are essential basic skills that all money-conscious gardeners should develop if they are not to waste unnecessary dollars on buying plants, or on buying plants whose only future is to languish and die.

Gardening on a Shoestring acts as a resource guide to help you find cheap materials and plants. It also details what to watch out for, and how to protect yourself from false bargains.

It encourages you to think laterally and to consider gardening and your garden in new ways. Plenty of cheap alternatives to conventional methods exist—all you need to do is step outside the frame to see them. Do you want fruit trees but find them too expensive? Share the purchase price with a neighbour, and plant on the boundary of your properties.

And finally, this book provides an introduction to other sources of information, because an educated gardener is a money-smart one. Garden clubs and societies, open gardens, government and semi-government instrumentalities, botanic gardens and radio talkback gardening programs all offer different kinds of money-saving resources and information.

You've taken the first step to becoming a money-smart gardener by picking up this book. Now read on, and start saving money.

CHAPTER 1

Self-Education

Gardening choices made through ignorance waste many, many thousands of dollars each year, but you needn't fall into the same trap. Learning as much as you can about gardening, and especially local conditions, will save you money.

Self-education prevents expensive mistakes. It means you won't choose plants that can't survive in your garden. Nor will you make costly landscaping blunders that cause flooding or damage to your house foundations (see Chapter 9). Best of all, self-education pays for itself not only in concrete monetary terms, but also in the rich satisfaction of widening your horizons and opening up the vast world of plants and gardening.

Your aim is, of course, to become a 'green thumb', to understand intuitively how to go about things in the garden so that plants thrive. Some years ago, my grandmother took a cutting of Lemon Verbena (*Aloysia triphylla*) and poked it roughly into the ground. A few months later it had struck and begun to grow. How did she know when to take the cutting, or how long to make it? How did she know it would strike so easily in ordinary garden soil? Had she read up on propagating Lemon Verbena in a book? I asked her. She laughed. 'No, of course not,' she said. But then how did she *know*? My grandmother merely shrugged. 'I just knew,' she said, and of course after fifty-plus years of observing and gardening and reading and propagating she did, indeed, 'just know'.

What Kind of Information Do You Need?

The information you need depends, of course, on how much you already know. For a complete beginner, though, I'd recommend several very basic spheres of knowledge that are easily picked up with a bit of reading, listening and looking.

Plant Biology

A basic understanding of plant biology will help you enormously. I've always believed that knowing *why* and *how* things work—the underlying processes and causes—provides a more reliable path to success than the rote learning of *whats* (such as lists of facts or superficial symptoms).

Understanding plant biology lets you diagnose problems through commonsense and deductive reasoning. Knowing only that the symptoms of nitrogen deficiency include yellow leaves is less useful than understanding that nitrogen is needed for the production of chlorophyll, which gives plants their green colour and which, in turn, is essential for the absorption of sunlight, and hence growth. Best of all, you won't waste money buying the wrong products; instead, you'll choose the right fertiliser for the right deficiency.

Learning about photosynthesis, germination, nutrient uptake, transpiration, pollination and other plant processes is nowhere near as daunting as it seems, because it's logical and interrelated. Just as we take a basic knowledge of human biology for granted (you know how the heart functions even though it's probably years since you read up on the circulatory system), you'll gradually absorb knowledge about plant biology, too. One day, six months to a year from the commencement of your investigations, you'll suddenly find yourself looking at a plant and seeing not only that it's lacking in vigour, but understanding why it's failing to thrive. Once you know why, the solution is rarely far away. And you'll save money because you'll need to replace fewer plants.

Plant Propagation

Plant propagation is a must-know for anyone who wants to save money in their garden and an overview is provided in Chapter 3.

Understanding plant biology makes propagation commonsense and very easy. When you know that seeds need certain temperature,

water and soil conditions to germinate, you're unlikely to plant them in an unsuitable medium or at the wrong time of year. You'll understand why vegetables fall into cool, warm and mid-season categories, so you won't waste money by planting tomatoes in the middle of a temperate winter. You'll understand how cuttings form roots and why you need to provide them with moisture *and* good drainage. And of course propagating your own plants will save you lots of money in the plant nursery.

Local Conditions

You should know the conditions in your garden, and you'll learn them through observation and commonsense. Is your climate tropical or temperate? Are there frosts? Do hot drying winds sweep through regularly? Is your soil acid or alkaline, clay or sand? Are there areas of poor drainage? Are certain insect or weed pests a problem in your region? When the weather forecast is read on the television or radio, do you need to add or subtract a few degrees? How quickly does your soil warm up in spring—should you delay planting by a few weeks because your garden is shaded, in a hollow, or on a south-facing slope? Is root competition from trees a problem?

This knowledge will help you choose

TIP

Secondary school textbooks (science and biology) are an excellent place to learn about basic plant biology, classification and nomenclature. Lower secondary science texts provide a more general overview than upper secondary biology texts. If you know a secondary school student, why not ask to borrow their textbook over the weekend to read the relevant chapters?

Photosynthesis is the conversion of carbon dioxide from the atmosphere to sugars within green parts of the plant, using chlorophyll (green pigment) and energy from sunlight.

Plant Propagation is the process of making new plants from old. You can easily make new plants by sowing seeds, taking cuttings (snipping off a part of the parent plant and treating it kindly so roots grow), dividing plants (separating pieces which already have roots), as well as by more complex techniques like budding, grafting and tissue culture.

TIP

Climate will determine what plants will grow in your garden. Plants adapted to **tropical** conditions (mild, dry winters and moist hot summers) often have large, glossy, soft green leaves. Most dislike cold, wet winters, are sensitive to frost, and scorch badly in hot, dry summers.

Many plants adapted to **temperate** conditions (hot dry summers and cold wet winters) succumb to fungal diseases when grown in tropical regions. Plants adapted to **arid** conditions (very hot and dry for most of the year) often have grey and/or furred leaves. They are susceptible to fungal disease if subjected to tropical summers or cold temperate winters.

plants that are suited to your site. The more suited the plants are to their environment, the less you'll spend on maintenance. And you won't waste money on plants that are condemned to die within a season.

Garden Design and Landscaping

Why does one garden look cluttered and unattractive and another beautiful? Unless you want to spend lots of money on the trial-and-error method of landscaping (when you rip out plants that prove unsuitable), it's a good idea read garden design books, visit open gardens, look at beautiful effects and identify why they work. Once again, it's better to understand principles of good design than to copy plant lists and combinations that are unlikely to translate effectively into your own garden when copied holus-bolus.

Plant Taxonomy

Of course, part of the fun of gardening is searching out and falling in love with new plants, so you'll also need a working knowledge of plant taxonomy, which is the classification of plants. Those Latin names are notoriously (and undeservedly) daunting to new gardeners. Fortunately, plant taxonomy is organised logically and you'll be amazed at what you already know (I'll bet you can already recognise roses, eucalypts, conifers, acacias and a whole host of other plant groups).

Those apparently complex botanical names are really no more difficult than our system of surnames and first names for people—you know that members of a family group often have the same surname, for example, so you don't need to remember the surname anew for each different member of the family you meet. Once you're familiar with plant names, the same applies.

The plant classification system of Kingdom, Division, Class, Order, Family, Genus and Species is analogous to an address: Planet Earth, Continent, State, City, Suburb, Street, and House number, so you know from the plant's name exactly where it fits in relation to other plants. You may even be able to glean an idea of its requirements, growth habits, and appearance. What springs to mind with the words *Eucalyptus leucoxylon*? You'll guess it's probably a tree, Australian, with sword-shaped grey-green leaves (you'd guess right). You'll probably know it has woody fruits, and you'll know more or less what the flowers look like. Not bad from two words. And a darn sight more information than you get from the name 'Fred Bloggs'.

Use correct botanical nomenclature whenever and as often you can, and the names will sink into your consciousness by themselves. It's not pretentious, but practical (common names of plants vary from region to region and person to person, and are unreliable and confusing—just try going into a nursery and asking for a Star Flower. You could walk out with any one of a dozen plants, from a climber to a tree to a small annual).

Best of all, you don't even need to worry about pronunciation when you use botanical names because all the Romans are dead.

Plant Classification

A number of different systems exist for the classification of living things, but all systems are based on the hierarchical system devised by Swedish naturalist Carolus Linnaeus in the eighteenth century.

One of the simplest classification systems recognises three KINGDOMS:
   Animalia (animals)
   Monera (bacteria and blue-green algae)
   Plantae (plants)

Gardeners cultivate plants.
   Each kingdom is subdivided into categories called DIVISIONS. For plants:
   Bryophyta (liverworts, mosses, hornworts)
   Chlorophyta (green algae)
   Chrysophyta (yellow-green algae, golden-brown algae and diatoms)
   Euglenophyta (euglenoids)
   Eumycophyta (true fungi)
   Myxomycophyta (slime molds)
   Phaeophyta (brown algae)
   Pyrrophyta (dinoflagellates)
   Rhodophyta (red algae)
   Tracheophyta (vascular plants)

Most gardeners grow vascular plants.
   Each division is further divided. For vascular plants, the categories are called SUB-DIVISIONS:
   Equisetopsida (horsetails)
   Filicopsida (true ferns)
   Lycopsida (club mosses)
   Magnoliopsida (seed plants)
   Psilotopsida (*Psilotum, Tmesipteris*)

Most cultivated garden plants are seed plants.
   Each division or subdivision is divided into categories called CLASSES. For seed plants:
   Angiospermae (flowering plants)
   Coniferae (conifers)
   Cycadae (cycads)
   Ginkgoae (*Ginkgo*)
   Gnetae (*Gnetum, Ephedra, Welwitschia*)
   Pteridospermae (seed ferns—extinct)

The vast majority of cultivated garden plants are flowering plants.
   The class Angiospermae is divided into two categories called SUBCLASSES:
   Dicotyledoneae (dicots)
   Monocotyledoneae (monocots)

Gardeners grow both monocots and dicots.
   The subclasses are further divided into categories called FAMILIES. For the subclass Monocotyledoneae, these include:
   Alliaceae
   Araceae
   Arecaceae
   Cyperaceae
   Hyacinthaceae
   Orchidaceae
   Poaceae
   and many more.

Each family is further divided into categories called GENERA (singular GENUS). For Cyperaceae, these include:
   Carex
   Cyperus
   Eleocharis
   Eriophorum
   Isolepis
   Schoenoplectus
   Uncinia

Each genus is divided into SPECIES. For *Carex*:

Carex albula
Carex elata
Carex flagellifera
Carex morrowii
and many more

The Names of Plants
The **botanical name** of a plant is the genus name and the species name, written in italics:

Genus species
e.g.
Lavandula angustifolia
Lavandula dentata
Lavandula viridis

The botanical name is a universal language for scientists, ensuring the same plant has the same name in every country in the world and allowing communication between botanists, plant breeders and gardeners.

The **common name** is a name used for the plant by non-botanists. Common names vary between people, regions and countries. In literature, a plant's common name (if it has one) and its botanical name are often both included, with the second in parentheses:

Genus species (Common Name)
OR
Common Name (*Genus species*)

A single common name may apply to one or more different species:

Lavandula angustifolia (English Lavender)
Lavandula × *intermedia* (English Lavender)

Alternatively, a single popular species may be known by several different common names:

Lavandula stoechas (Spanish Lavender, French Lavender, Italian Lavender)

Rare, uncommonly cultivated and new plants may have no common name:

Lavandula latifolia

In a list of plants all of which are in the same genus, the genus is often abbreviated after the first mention in full:

Lavandula angustifolia
L. dentata
L. stoechas

A single unnamed or unknown species is denoted by the abbreviation sp.:

Lavandula sp.

Two or more species in the same genus are collectively denoted by the abbreviation spp.:

Lavandula spp.

A **hybrid** (a genetic cross between two different species) is identified by an × between the genus and species:

Lavandula × *intermedia*

A **cultivar** is a **cul**tivated **var**iety of a species, often an improved version with more, larger or longer lasting blooms or fruit, produced by plant breeders, and is written thus:

Lavandula angustifolia 'Munstead'

A **subspecies** is the rank in plant classification below species. It applies usually to a wild population that is significantly and consistently different in one particular geographical region from populations of the same species growing elsewhere. It is written thus:

Lavandula stoechas subsp. *lusitanica*
or, in a list
L. stoechas. subsp. *lusitanica*

Plant Identification

Knowing and understanding botanical nomenclature is important for gardeners, but being able to *recognise* plants has obvious benefits, too. Learn by being observant, by asking, by taking pieces home and looking them up in books (believe me, once you've spent three hours combing your bookshelves to identify a plant, you won't forget its name *or* its appearance!).

Plant Maintenance and Improving Microclimate

Fertilisers, pesticides, drainage, mulching, composting, windbreaks and pruning all fall into the category of plant maintenance and improving microclimate. Most of these techniques are covered in this book, but your expertise will also build with time, especially if you keep your eyes, ears and mind open. The very fact you're reading this book suggests you're well on the way to gaining these skills.

Where to Find Information

Sources of information are all around you, and most of the sources are free or very cheap.

Garden Clubs (see Appendix 5 for a list)
Garden clubs are excellent sources of information. You'll hear talks, visit gardens, see slides, exchange or buy plants at trading tables, and meet plenty of nice people.

Garden clubs can be split into the three following categories.

1. **Plant societies** focus on specific plant groups, such as irises or roses. Capital cities may even boast two societies for the one plant group, and large regional centres may have one too. These clubs are great for specific information if you develop a passion for any particular plant, but you'll also find members who attend other garden clubs so there's a cross-fertilisation of ideas so to speak.
2. **'Friends of' clubs** are associated with a botanic, community or heritage garden. If the focus garden is in your local area, you'll learn a lot about local conditions, as well as helping an invariably cash-strapped organisation as a volunteer.
3. **District garden clubs** are the ones in your local area. These are the best bet for learning about local conditions, and you'll make lots of friends in your area. District clubs are especially useful if you live in a difficult area (near the seaside, with low rainfall, or a in a frost pocket).

You can find details of meeting times in your local newspaper, in gardening magazines, and on radio and television gardening programs. Botanic gardens often provide listings of groups too.

Botanic Gardens (see Appendix 3 for details)
Botanic gardens are ideal for learning plant names, because specimens are usually labelled and beds are often laid out into genera or families. This gives you a 'feel' for groups of plants and their growth habits, especially if you revisit the garden in different seasons.

Many botanic gardens showcase water gardens, rockeries, woodlands, shadehouses and glasshouses, providing you with ideas for different areas of your garden. There may be delightful interpretive walking trails, with brochures or maps describing the plants you see, or guided walks at designated times. Ring up to get a brochure on monthly events—lots are free.

Some botanic gardens provide a home gardens advisory service, often associated with a herbarium, so for the price of a telephone call you'll get advice on growing a particular plant species. Or drop in to have plants identified, but beware—the garden's

> ### TIP
> Visiting the library? Look for
> books about gardening around
> Call No. 635, garden design around
> 712, and plants/botany around 581.

shop usually stocks a mouth-watering array of gorgeous plant books, so leave your credit card behind if you're serious about saving money. Luckily, the shops also stock cheap or free pamphlets and fliers written by botanists and horticulturalists, specifically for growing plants in *local* conditions.

Libraries

Libraries are free and most boast a very reasonable gardening section. I'm an author so admit to some bias, but I believe books are the ideal place to learn about gardening. Books describe every conceivable aspect of plants and gardening, from propagation to design, from simple how-tos to academic texts on plant biochemistry, from glossy hardbacks with inspiring photos, to information-packed paperbacks. Libraries also carry a range of gardening magazines, so you can drop in each month if you want to save a few extra dollars.

Local Councils

Most local councils provide free brochures about problem plants such as those that should be avoided near plumbing and foundations; bird- or bee-attracting plants that should not be planted near pools; and so on. They'll also tell you about good-neighbour plants, and legal responsibilities with regard to fencing, pruning, run-off and tree-lopping.

Some councils own neighbourhood houses with attached community gardens, where you can learn from other gardeners while developing your skills.

Government Organisations (see Appendix 4 for details)

Many Departments of Health, Electricity, Water, Agriculture, and Forestry provide lists of plants suited to bushfire-prone areas, pest plants, and plants to avoid near power lines or septic systems. Some provide information on pesticides, horticulture and weed control. In some areas, Country Fire Service officers will come to your house and advise on planting and bushfire protection.

Local Newspapers

Although national papers contain weekly gardening columns, the state and local ones supply seasonal information about planting crops and 'jobs to do in the garden this week'. They advertise local garden clubs and shows, too, as well as sales at garden centres and nurseries.

Horticulture Courses

Horticulture courses include community workshops, accredited university and TAFE certificates and diplomas, and adult education courses (see Appendix 2). Courses range from three-hour plant propagation courses to weekend cottage gardening sessions to two- or three-year qualifications in general horticulture, green-keeping, landscaping, and more.

Plant Nurseries

Don't bail up the proprietor or staff for too long (especially if they're busy), but if you're a regular buying customer nursery people should be happy to give you advice on planting, especially if it applies to specimens you've bought from them in the first place.

Magazines

There's a range of magazines available, varying in price, quality and content. Some are crammed with glossy pictures but are light on information; others are targeted at experienced horticulturists, others at rich people (you can recognise them by their advertisements for exorbitantly priced garden sculptures, ceramic dinnerware and bed-and-breakfast country getaways).

Television and Radio

These are entertaining and can be informative, but beware. Radio programs, especially regional ones, vary enormously in the quality of their advice. Gardening's a bit like raising children: though certain basic rules apply, everyone has their own methods. Time and time again I've heard gardening talkback hosts give wrong information to callers. In one instance, the host suggested a herbicide that would be completely ineffective on the weed plaguing the caller's garden. Worse, the host did not pass on this information even after I rang and spoke to him off-air. The hapless caller no doubt wasted her money at the garden centre that very day.

The Internet

The Internet carries a vast amount of gardening information, though if you're a bit of a Luddite like me you'll find the sheer volume of data bewildering (about 46,000 matches came up when I searched for 'gardening'!). You can look up Web Sites and Pages for gardening, plants, design and many specific garden-related products and areas, or join chat lines where you exchange information and gossip with other gardeners.

CHAPTER 2

Buying Cheaper Plants

One of the major costs in creating a garden is, of course, plants, and all keen gardeners know how tempting it is to splurge on these. Unfortunately, impulse buying is just as dangerous in the nursery as in the supermarket, and you can easily find yourself returning home with boxes of large trees for a small inner city garden, or tropical species when you live in a frost hollow. Beware! And although gardens have distinct boundaries and seem to conform to the usual laws of geometry, in reality they are more like Dr Who's Tardis: every gardener knows that there is *always* room for one more plant!

However, let's assume your garden is not hopelessly overplanted but comprises instead a large expanse of bare soil. If you're serious about saving money you'll propagate as many plants as possible yourself (see Chapter 3), but there are many instances where you'll want or need to *buy* plants.

Why **Buy** Plants at All?

Some plants are difficult to propagate. The seeds of certain Australian native species need special treatment before they'll germinate; others germinate very slowly (taking a year or more) or take a long time to reach flowering size (see pp. 34–5).

Other plants strike from cuttings but require special (and expensive) equipment like hot benches or mist irrigation to do so. Some plants are notoriously slow-growing (Black Mondo Grass, Tree Paeony, Sweet Bay), and it may be worth paying a little extra for a larger plant that won't disappear amongst the weeds or be inadvertently trampled.

Some plants are temperamental when small, dying suddenly and for no apparent reason. So it's best to buy them when they're larger and more reliable.

It may not be possible to find seed or cutting material of more unusual plants. And grafted/budded cultivars often perform poorly when grown as cuttings on their own roots, so unless you've done some budding and grafting yourself, it's better to leave this to the experts.

Before You Buy

Browse wherever plants are sold. Get a feel for prices so you'll recognise a good deal when you see one. Prices vary with pot size (larger pots are usually, but not always, more expensive) and with plant species (certain plants, like camellias, rhododendrons and conifers, cost more to produce and are therefore more expensive to buy). Not surprisingly, classy garden centres with high overheads in up-market suburbs are often more expensive than slightly grungy outer-suburbs nurseries. Don't be sucked in by fancy presentation—you're buying the plant in the pot, not the paving, pergolas, archways and standard roses around the car park.

You'll succumb to impulse buying now and then, but if you're serious about saving money it's better to visit a nursery with a clear idea of what kind of plant you want (tree, shrub, groundcover or annual), so you don't come home with boxes of plants you don't really need.

TIP

Buying jointly is a great option if your relationship with your neighbours is a good long-term one and you want to plant expensive fruit tree cultivars or varieties that require cross-pollination (i.e. you need to buy two trees if they're to fruit well).

In the case of trees that need cross-pollination (e.g. some cherries, persimmons, plums), rather than buying both specimens yourself and cramming them into your garden, you and your neighbour can buy one each—half the cost, but plenty of fruit on each of your trees.

Alternatively, you can each pay half the purchase price of a self-pollinating tree and plant it on your boundary, so that you and your neighbour harvest fruit from half of the tree respectively. This is particularly effective if your boundary runs north–south; east–west boundaries can be less fair because many fruit plants tend to bear more heavily on the northern side of the tree. Take care with boundary plantings to ensure fences aren't damaged, and be aware that if your neighbour moves away all bets are off.

Where to Buy Cheap Plants

Nurseries and garden centres aren't the only or the cheapest places to buy plants. **Trash-and-treasure markets** and **school fetes** almost always include plant stalls. Plants are usually very cheap and you may be able to negotiate a discount if you're buying lots. You can often get seed at excellent prices, too, but check that it's been collected recently and is not too old.

If you're looking for a wide selection of plants, arrive early (*very* early) because many of the choice specimens will be snapped up quickly (often by other stallholders!). If you just want to buy cheap, go late in the day, just before pack-up time, and haggle. If you don't mind getting lumbered with a few plants you don't actually like, you can sometimes get a good deal by making an offer to cart away *all* the leftovers.

Some small nurseries regularly attend trash-and-treasure markets. Be aware that, unlike backyard or hobby operators, the stall-holders' livelihoods are at stake, and they operate on a small profit margin. Follow your own conscience by all means, but I think that under these circumstances it is mean-spirited to beat down the price, which is generally low anyway.

Many **garden clubs** and **plant societies** run trading tables at their monthly meetings (see Appendix 5). Plants are usually cheap and healthy, and you'll be able to get cultural instructions direct from the grower. Annual plant fairs run by larger societies (such as the Society for Growing Australian Plants (SGAP), the Herb Society and the Camellia Society) are also excellent but, once again, it's best to arrive early. Prices tend to be slightly higher than at trading tables, but lower than what you'd pay at a commercial nursery.

You can sometimes pick up great bargains at **house demolition sales** when established plants (especially bulbs and clumping perennials like agapanthus) are dug up and sold, often in large numbers.

What to Watch Out For

Poor Labelling

Buying at fetes and trash-and-treasure markets is cheap but it can also be a bit of a lucky dip—plants are rarely labelled or, if they are, are often labelled incorrectly. Asking the stallholder may or may not be of use. Better to have a gardening friend accompany you. Otherwise the small shrub you bought for that tight corner will reach 8 metres and crack the foundations of your house, rather negating the bargain you thought you had!

Old Seed

Make sure that seeds bought at markets are reasonably fresh and viable. The crispness of the envelope is usually a good indication of how long the seed's been around; avoid anything that looks as if it's been stored since 1948 in a damp corner of someone's potting shed (see p. 34 for storing and sowing seed).

Contaminated Potting Mix

Plants bought at fetes have often been potted in garden soil. If you buy regularly from markets, you'll eventually end up with a garden that contains not only every plant in the area but also every *weed* and soil-borne disease as well! Obviously, you should avoid buying plants that are accompanied by a generous selection of weed seedlings. If you must have the plant and it's a reasonably hardy variety, it's worth upending the pot when you get home and shaking the excess soil from the roots. *Discard this soil*; don't put it into your compost heap. Rinse any remaining soil from the roots, then repot the plant into your own potting mix or garden soil, or plant direct into the garden. Give the plant plenty of TLC while the roots reestablish.

Diseased Stock

Although it's fine to buy pot-bound plants that often look a little hungry and parched, you should *never* buy diseased stock. (Pot-bound plants look hungry, thirsty and stunted with yellowing leaves. Diseased plants will have yellow stripes or spots on the leaves; cracks in the bark; lots of dead tips to the branches; twisted, gnarled growth or thickening of parts of the stem, branches, leaves or flowers; or show obvious signs of insect infestation.)

Buying at Nurseries and Garden Centres

Seeds

Seeds are certainly the cheapest way to produce large numbers of plants.

Annuals

Annuals are much cheaper when bought as packets of seeds than as punnets of seedlings. If you're reading this book you shouldn't even *think* of buying annuals in pots. And if you're serious about saving money, you should grow nearly all vegetables and annual flowers only from seeds—you'll save heaps (see p. 32 for growing plants from seed).

Value for Money

When buying seed, compare value for money as you would potato chips in a supermarket. Calculate weight/number of seeds per dollar, and don't be deceived by the size of the outer packaging (like potato chip manufacturers,

Annuals are plants that grow and flower in one year or less and then die.

Biennials live for two years only. They usually flower and seed in their second year, though some flower in their first year as well.

Perennials are plants that live for more than three years.

seed suppliers often put a tiny foil sachet of seed in a paper envelope five times the size!).

Viability

Check the use-by date and that the seed packets don't look excessively dusty or faded (viability will decrease if seeds have been exposed to extremes of temperature). Vacuum-packed seed retains its viability longer.

The large commercial seed suppliers produce viable and reliable seed, and you can expect a good germination rate from them when you buy their products at nurseries. Buy carefully from smaller seed suppliers, especially if you're going direct to the supplier (usually mail-order). Avoid like the plague those gimmicky seeds produced by marketing people (as opposed to horticulturists)—the seeds are usually hugely expensive and packaged in a capsule or bubble mounted on a large and glossy rectangle of cardboard. The illustration is usually wildly unrepresentative and the enclosed species is all too often notorious for its nonviable/difficult-to-germinate seed.

Seedlings

Seedlings are more expensive than seed, but cheaper than annuals in pots (the least cost-effective way of buying annuals).

Germination is the active growth of an embryo resulting in the development of a young plant.

The term 'viability' when used to describe seeds refers to whether the seeds are alive or dead. Seeds must be viable to germinate.

Germination rate refers to the percentage of seeds sown that germinate into seedlings. Old seeds and seeds that have been improperly stored often have a poor germination rate.

Seedlings are immature plants grown from seed. They are usually sold in punnets (shallow square or rectangular pots), with multiple (six, nine, twelve or more) individual seedlings or clumps of seedlings in each punnet. Choose punnets with the most and the healthiest seedlings to get best value for money.

Number of Seedlings

Once again, check number of *plants* per punnet; sometimes seed has been sown direct or seedlings pricked out as small clumps rather than individually. By carefully separating the seedlings at home, you get not the dozen you've paid for, but twenty or even thirty plants. Because you've disturbed the roots, you'll need to give the separated seedlings extra care while they're establishing, but most common flowers and herbs are hardy enough to survive this treatment.

Perennial Savings

Buying perennial herbs (e.g. oreganos, thymes) and flowers (chrysanthemums, asters) in punnets is excellent value for money (one punnet is about half the price of a standard-size pot and you'll get at least six plants, not one).

TIP

When choosing seedlings, don't go for the tallest ones. Bigger is *not* better when buying seedlings. Choose instead the slightly smaller, more compact ones—they haven't been sitting around in the garden centre for as long, are easier to handle (and to separate if necessary), and will grow away more vigorously. Look for good colour (not too many yellow leaves) and healthy shooting buds (active growth and small leaves at the tips).

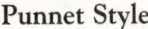

Punnet Style

Punnets that comprise individual mini-pots minimise root disturbance but are often slightly more expensive than the old-fashioned flat-bottomed rectangular or square punnet.

Mail-order Plants

Most mail-order nurseries (many specialising in **herbaceous** or **deciduous perennials**) are generous with their plants. They're often grown in the open ground, then dug while they're dormant, so the grower needs no pots or potting mix. Instead, the plants are packed in peat moss and/or sawdust, wrapped in plastic and/or newspaper and mailed to customers. The clumps that you receive may well be divisible several times (see pp. 30–1 on how to divide plants)— why not share the cost and the plant with another gardener? For those plants that can't be divided, why not exchange pieces after they've been in your garden for a season?

Potted Plants

Potted plants are expensive when compared with seeds and punnets of seedlings, but you may have no choice: some plants are sold only as potted specimens. Still, it's possible to get bargains here too. The trick is to know what to buy and when. Many plants can be divided straight from the pot, so you get two, four or even ten for the price of one! (See pp. 30–2 for easy-to-divide plants.) You can also take advantage of nursery sales and discounts, and choose pot sizes that are the best value for money.

Sales

Nurseries and garden centres regularly hold sales and advertise discount offers, and you can take advantage of these by watching for advertisements in local newspapers.

Herbaceous perennials are perennials with non-woody stems. Although herbaceous perennials originating in Europe or North America are deciduous in icy Northern Hemisphere winters, many are evergreen or only briefly or partly deciduous in Australia's milder climate.

Deciduous plants are those that lose their leaves in winter in temperate climates. They may be herbaceous (non-woody like asters and hellebores) or woody (e.g. roses, maples, *Forsythia* and currants). In many plant books, 'herbaceous' and 'deciduous' are used interchangeably to describe perennials.

Evergreen perennials don't lose their leaves or go dormant. They may be woody (e.g. camellias, eucalypts), or non-woody (e.g. *Agapanthus*, Kangaroo Paw).

Discounts

If you're buying a lot of plants, and the nursery is a small one that propagates its own plants and also wholesales, you can ask for a discount of, say, 10 per cent on the retail price (the wholesale price is about 50 per cent of the retail price so the proprietor will still make a good profit on her sale to you). You're unlikely to get a discount from a nursery that does not propagate its own stock but buys it all in.

Bargains

Many nurseries have a bargains table. The table may display annuals past their best (usually not worth buying unless there's plenty of seed forming) or plants that have missed a watering (a great bargain as most respond well to TLC—just look for new green growth at the tips or leaf axils to be sure your plant will respond). Often you'll also see pot-bound plants that the grower has decided to sell off cheaply rather than to pot into bigger containers. There's a myth that you should never buy pot-bound plants but, like all urban myths, this is rubbish. Nearly all pot-bound plants thrive when planted in the garden, providing you first tease out the

TIP

Many Australian native plants are grown in tubes and are available at cheap prices from the Society for Growing Australian Plants (SGAP) at their sales.

A **rhizome** is a stem that creeps on or below the soil surface, forming roots as it goes. Rhizomes are often thickened (either fleshy or hard and woody), storing food for over-wintering perennials.

roots a little or score (slice or cut shallowly) the outside of the rootball with a sharp knife. The plants may look a little straggly and 'leggy' at first, and take a bit longer to establish in the garden, but give them good soil, plenty of fertiliser and a good prune and they'll thrive.

The only pot-bound plants to avoid are citrus, certain species that resent root disturbance, and seed-grown shrubs and trees, especially native species. Unlike cutting-grown plants, which form a fibrous root mass, seed-grown plants often have a long taproot which winds around itself in a tight spiral or knot when kept too long in a small container. The plants grow well initially, but have a nasty habit of blowing over in the garden just when they're tall enough to do some damage.

Pot Size

Nurseries that propagate their own stock usually make cuttings into tubes and then, when they've struck roots, 'pot on' into larger pots. The tubes are rarely displayed for sale, but some nurseries will let you buy them, especially if you want lots. Tube stock is about half the price of potted stock. If you're wanting fifty-plus plants for a mass display or hedge, you can ask such a nursery to propagate the plants for you, but be prepared to pay a generous deposit.

It makes good sense to buy fast-growing species as tube stock rather than in pots (or in small pots as opposed to larger ones),

because after one season's growth in the garden both plants will be of comparable size.

Dividing Potted Plants

Plants that can be divided may be good value in pots (see pp. 30–1 for easy-to-divide plants). Rather than buying three pots, you can buy a single well-established one, tip out the plant, and slice it vertically into thirds or quarters (as you would a round cake). Many plants can be divided this way (indeed, nurseries often use this technique to maintain their own stock).

Mat-forming Groundcovers

Many carpeting groundcovers that form a mat are easy to divide (see p. 30 for a list). Just check that the plant has actually formed roots along its trailing branches (i.e. it is attached all over the surface of the potting soil) and is not in fact just lying on the surface with a central stem. Once again, be aware that because you've disturbed the roots, you'll need to give the plants extra water and care during the establishment phase.

Clump-forming Plants with Grassy Leaves

Most clump-forming species with grassy leaves also generally divide easily (see p. 31 for easy-to-divide clump-forming plants). In this case, you should buy a pot with as many sprouts as possible (check near the base, where the leaves disappear into the soil). Then, depending on the toughness of the plant, you can separate the pieces by pulling, cutting with a sharp knife or, for large plants with woody rhizomes, hacking with a spade, saw or axe (see Chapter 3 for more details on propagation).

Herbaceous Perennials

Many **herbaceous perennials** actually grow better if they're divided regularly (see p. 31 for easy-to-divide herbaceous perennials). Once again, look for a full pot. Ideally, you should divide these when they're dormant (usually late autumn to early spring), but it's easiest when you can see the side plants actively sprouting and they're a reasonable size to handle. If you're buying herbaceous perennials in the height of their growing season, you can plant them, enjoy the flowers, and then lift and divide them, but you don't have to wait until then. Contrary to popular belief, you can divide herbaceous perennials pretty well at any time of year, though they'll scorch in summer and take longer to recover if you do it as they're coming into flower (and the flowers suffer too).

Bare-rooted Bargains

Deciduous Trees

Deciduous trees are available all year round in pots, but they're much cheaper bought bare-rooted (i.e. with their roots bare of soil) in winter. Such trees are grown in the open ground for a season or three until they're of saleable size, and 'dug' in early winter after they've lost their leaves and their fine feeder roots. The trees survive bare-rooted because they're dormant: without leaves they tran-

> ### TIP
> Need four plants of the same variety? Don't buy four pots if the plant is divisible. Instead, choose one full pot and divide into four at one-quarter the price.

spire no water. After digging the trees, the wholesale nursery then trucks them to retail outlets, where they're displayed with their roots covered with damp sawdust or sand to prevent them from drying out. You choose *and plant* bare-rooted deciduous trees before they come into leaf.

You'll need to know what you want because bare-root deciduous trees all look the same (a bunch of kindling wood), so work out what kind of tree you'd like during summer or autumn. There are two exceptions: certain seed-grown, autumn-foliage trees whose colour varies enormously (e.g. liquidambars) and trees that are notoriously unreliable when bought dormant (e.g. persimmons). You should buy these trees potted and in leaf (in autumn when they're in full colour for foliage trees) so you can be sure you've got a good, healthy specimen.

Roses

Roses are much cheaper bare-rooted too, and there's always a label with a photograph so you know what you're getting. I'd recommend against paying full-price for bare-rooted roses that have been kept at the supermarket too long and have come into full leaf, but if they're being sold off cheaply they're an excellent bargain. Contrary to popular advice, they'll survive if you give them plenty of TLC and acclimatise them by planting them into a pot in a shady, sheltered site (don't put them straight into a hot, windy spot). You might need to trim soft, wilty growth, but once the plants are established in the pots you can move them into progressively more exposed positions until you plant them into the ground in their final position.

Bulbs

Avoid buying bulbs in full flower in fancy pots from garden centres and nurseries (though you can sometimes pick up bargains when the bulb has finished flowering and is

TIP

Supermarket Bulb Bargains
You can sometimes get fantastic bulb bargains at supermarkets. Once packaged bulbs have begun to sprout, they're often sold off at incredibly low prices because managers assume these bulbs aren't likely to survive. Wrong. Just check there's no sign of mould, rot or mildew, then buy your bargain, take it home and plant into a pot filled with good quality, well-drained potting mix. Put the pot in a sheltered but well-ventilated spot while the roots establish.

looking a bit yellow as it goes into its dormant phase). Bulbs are usually cheapest bought from specialist mail-order suppliers. If you can arrange to buy jointly you'll make further savings because most such suppliers offer discounts for larger quantities.

Bargain-hunting Checklist

There are always exceptions, but if you want to save money your best bet will be to buy:
- **annuals** (including vegetables) as seed
- **bulbs** when they're dormant
- **deciduous trees** (including fruit trees) and roses bare-rooted in winter
- **fast-growing shrubs** and trees (especially **Australian natives**) as tube stock
- **herbaceous perennials** from mail-order nurseries
- **perennial plants** as seedlings (look for full punnets)

When buying potted plants:
- ask for **discounts** when buying multiples of one plant
- ask for **tube stock**
- check the **bargains table**
- **divide** any plants that can be divided (look for full pots)
- take advantage of **sales** at nurseries and garden centres

CHAPTER 3

Propagating Your Own Plants

Propagating your own plants is one of the most effective ways of saving money in your garden, and it's addictive. There's something enormously satisfying in producing your own plants, whether it be from seed, cuttings, division or any other technique, and once you learn the skills you will never again be limited to the garden centre. See a plant you like? Beg, borrow or steal a small piece or some seed and one to six months later you'll have a plant of your own.

Best of all, you can propagate your own berries, vegetables and culinary herbs, thereby saving money not only in the garden, but also at the greengrocer (see Easy-to-propagate Culinary Herbs on p. 39).

The simplest forms of plant propagation require no special training. Instructions are printed on the back of seed packets, division is idiot-proof, and cuttings of easy-to-strike plants grow practically where they're thrown (remember the pieces of ivy and *Tradescantia* forming roots in a jar of water on the kitchen windowsill?). Many plants may be propagated by simple techniques, and merely by reading this chapter you'll gain the skills to propagate them.

Other plants (especially cultivars of fruit trees and roses) require more specialised methods. Budding and grafting are two skills that are best learned when you clearly understand the plant biology involved, and I recommend hands-on practice with an expert grafter. You can also buy or borrow books dealing with propagation in more detail than I have the space to go into here.

If you plan to propagate most of your own plants, or if you have a large property to green, you should consider enrolling in one of the many plant propagation courses offered by adult education institutes (see Appendix 2 for addresses), nurseries, garden clubs and private individuals around Australia. The courses range from intensive weekend workshops to three-year diplomas, and vary correspondingly in price. Still, you'll recoup the cost in your first year of propagating if you need a lot of plants.

Alternatively, you can spend a week or two of work experience at a plant nursery—nearly all the techniques you'll use are simple and straightforward, and don't require exceptionally honed fine motor skills (this from an experienced propagator who has rotten ones!).

What You'll Need

The basic tools for propagating plants are precisely what you'd expect: containers, soil/mix to go in them, simple climate controls to provide moisture and to protect delicate new plants from extremes of climate, and implements to cut, insert, or sow the plants. Of course, many expensive propagating aids are available: special heated trays, misters, tubes, propagating media, sterilisers and so on. Fortunately, you don't need to buy any of them, although if you're planning on propagating hundreds of plants (seed or cuttings) at a time, it will be cost-effective to buy containers. There are cheap alternatives around if you're prepared to spend a little extra time on preparation.

Recycled Containers

For propagating, all containers should be very clean because fungi and bacteria can devastate a crop of germinating seeds or cuttings. It's fine to recycle old pots, but give them a thorough scrub in detergent and a bleach solution. Let them dry thoroughly before use. And if you don't have access to pots, don't despair. With minor modifications, many plastic household containers are ideal for propagating seed and cuttings (see p. 58 for ideas). Polystyrene boxes used by greengrocers are excellent for large numbers of plants.

For cuttings, you can buy second-hand tubes from nurseries.

Extra Cover

Seeds

Seeds need warmth to germinate. You can increase warmth and humidity around your seeds by covering the seed tray with a **pane of glass or black plastic** (but in hot conditions be sure to remove it as soon as the seedlings emerge or you'll cook them).

Cuttings

Most leafy cuttings need a higher humidity than is provided by the open air in

TIP

Cuttings of plants with very soft, furry/woolly, fleshy or grey-coloured leaves (e.g. some pelargoniums, saltbushes, and Lamb's Ears) often rot if humidity is high and do better without a covering.

Australia's warm temperate climate: moisture is lost from the leaves faster than it can be drawn up by the cut bottom-end of the stem, and the leaves wilt badly. Humidity around cuttings can be increased by covering the container with an inverted **plastic bag** supported by two or three sticks or bent wires inserted into the pot. Snip the corners of the bag or raise the lower edges a little where they meet the pot to ensure adequate ventilation (if there's not enough, you'll have problems with fungi).

'Bottom heat' speeds root growth of many cuttings and can also speed germination. If you own an **outdoor water heater** in a sheltered and well-lit spot, you can place trays of cuttings on top of the unit. I also know one propagator who places her trays of seed and cuttings in an old electric frypan set to its lowest temperature and lined with pebbles!

Miscellaneous Tools

You'll need a **watering can**, sprayer or hose nozzle that has a fine setting. For smoothing seed-raising mix before sowing, you'll need a **wooden block** (or any hard, smooth object, like a half-brick, tile, or small box).

Strike means the emergence of roots of a cutting (you can 'strike' cuttings, and when the roots emerge a cutting is said to have 'struck').

Callus is undifferentiated cell growth which precedes the emergence of roots of a cutting.

TIP

Homemade Propagating Mixes

Use well-rotted, sieved compost or manure sterilised in the oven or microwave. Fresh manures, especially 'hot' ones like poultry and pigeon, will burn the delicate roots and emerging shoots of seedlings. Old, well-rotted cow manure is excellent but should be sterilised. Add about two-thirds (by volume) of washed river sand or sharp sand for drainage.

Avoid substituting washed or sharp sand with ordinary builders' sand. Builders' sand is fine and dusty, and the tiny particles will clog your mix and block drainage holes in containers.

To make holes for cuttings in the propagating mix, you'll need a **dibber** (a pointed length of dowel the approximate size of a pencil—in fact, a pencil will do very well).

The only tool for which there is no effective substitute is a damn good pair of **secateurs**. Keep them clean and sharp and they'll last for years. They'll also improve your success rate when propagating cuttings because any cuts you make will be neat, will callus more quickly, and will be less vulnerable to infection. Oh, and that applies to your fingers, too.

Sharp sand comes from crushing operations at quarries. The particles are angular and 'sharp' and improve aeration and drainage in mixes, as well as promoting root formation of cuttings. The sand may contain fine materials that need to be washed out.

Washed river sand has smoother, rounded particles that promote aeration and drainage, and that are excellent in media for seedlings or plants that need particularly good drainage.

Propagating Mixes

Propagating mix should be sterile. You can make up your own blends using combinations of commercial mixes and compost from home (see Tip on this page), but you'll need to sterilise home brews in the oven or microwave to kill any bugs.

Seed-Raising Mixes

Seed-raising mixes should be light, fine, crumbly/friable and free-draining. Commercial mixes usually contain **perlite**, which resembles bean-bag balls at first glance but which is in fact a heat-treated volcanic rock. It's very light, but with excellent water-holding capacity (about 25 per cent). Many propagating mixes also contain **washed river sand** or **vermiculite** (a heat-treated mineral like perlite, similarly light but able to hold about 50 per cent water), plus a little **peat**. You can buy these ingredients separately and mix them with either ordinary potting mix or your own compost—remember that you're aiming for a light texture and good water retention without waterlogging. **Two classic time-proven propagating blends are 75 per cent river sand with 25 per cent peat moss for seed, and equal parts river sand, loam and leaf mould/peat for seedlings.**

Once wetted, the medium should allow the water to drain immediately and freely, without sitting on the surface for more than a few seconds. Drainage holes should not become blocked by fine materials washing through the medium. After watering, a handful of medium should yield water when squeezed, but not as much as a sponge of the same size! Certain species will need a wetter mix than others (e.g. ferns versus arid-zone plants), so experiment.

Cutting Mixes

Media for cuttings vary with the type of plant and season (you'll need slightly more sand or aerating ingredient in the mixture during wet times of the year), but usually contain sharp sand or perlite, and peat. Sharp sand is particularly good for striking cuttings. A standard mix is:

- one-third to one-half peat (or fine, well-rotted compost or equivalent)
- two-thirds to one-half sand (or perlite or equivalent) by volume

A time-proven blend for cuttings is equal parts river sand, perlite and peat moss. All are good and you can adapt your mix according to the availability and cost of ingredients (perlite is expensive).

If you're not sure about the suitability of your cutting mix, you can check by watering; the general requirements are as for seed-raising mix, but drainage is even more important. If in doubt, err on the side of a drier (freer draining) mix, with extra sand/perlite rather than peat or compost, because cuttings are susceptible to rotting.

Propagating Media for Division

When propagating bulbs and plants by division, you won't need fancy mixes, because roots are already developed. You can pot into ordinary potting mix (commercial, or a home blend as described on p. 29) or even straight into the garden.

Propagating Plants by Division

Division is easier than sowing seed, because unlike with seed or a cutting, you start with an entire plant in miniature: it has roots, stems and leaves—in fact, all the bits it needs to grow. Dividing a plant is just as it sounds: separating an established plant into two or more pieces.

You can divide mat-forming plants, clump-forming plants and herbaceous perennials.

When to Divide

In temperate climates, autumn and spring are good times to divide mat- or clump-forming evergreen perennials such as *Agapanthus*,

---

Easy-to-divide Mat-forming Plants

Arenaria caespitosa 'Aurea'
Arenaria montana
Ajuga reptans (Bugle Weed)
Chamaemelum nobile (Chamomile)
Gallium odoratum (Sweet Woodruff)
Gazania spp.
Heuchera sanguinea (Coral Bells)
Mentha spp. (mints)
Origanum spp. (oreganos)
Prunella vulgaris (Self Heal)
Saxifraga stolonifera
Sellieria radicans
Thymus spp. (thymes)
Viola odorata (Sweet Violets)

Clivea, *Gazania* and Sweet Violets. Avoid late autumn and winter in very cold, wet regions as plants may languish or rot and, if you can, the height of summer in hot areas, as plants take longer to recover.

A good rule of thumb for herbaceous perennials like asters, campanulas, *Echinacea* and Shasta Daisies is to divide spring-flowering ones in autumn or winter and summer- or autumn-flowering ones in spring (i.e. when active growth commences)—see Easy-to-divide Herbaceous Perennials on p. 31 for more.

Give divided plants a little extra TLC while they grow, being especially careful to keep the plants well watered until their roots are established.

How to Divide

Mat-forming Plants

1. Pull or cut pieces from established plant, ensuring each piece has roots.
2. For potted specimens, upend the pot and slice the plant vertically into halves, thirds or quarters. Replant into individual pots or soil.

Easy-to-divide Clump-forming Plants

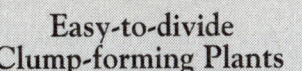

Agapanthus orientalis (African Lily)
Anigozanthos spp. (kangaroo paws)
Aristea spp.
Armeria maritima (Sea Thrift)
Aspidistra elatior (Aspidistra)
Clivea spp.
Dianella revoluta, D. tasmanica
Dierama pulcherrimum (Fairy Fishing Rods)
Dietes bicolor
Iris spp. (irises)
Kniphofia spp. (Red Hot Poker)
Libertia formosa
Ophiopogon citratus (Lemon Grass)
Poaceae (grasses including *Carex, Festuca, Iphiopogon, Restio*)
Schizostylis coccinea
Sisyrinchium spp.
Tulbaghia violacea (Society Garlic)

Easy-to-divide Herbaceous Perennials

Achillea spp. (yarrows)
Anemone japonica (Chinese Windflower)*
Aster spp. (Michaelmas Daisies)
Bletilla striata (Chinese Ground Orchid)*
Campanula spp. (bellflowers)
Coreopsis verticillata
Echinacea purpurea (Purple Coneflower)
Geum spp. (avens)
Hosta spp. (Plantain Lily)*
Leucanthemum × *superbum* (Shasta Daisy)
Lychnis chalcedonica (Maltese Cross)
Melissa officinalis (Lemon Balm)
Polygonatum multiflorum (Solomon's Seal)*
Tanacetum vulgare (Tansy)
Veronica spicata (Speedwell)
* These plants have entirely below-ground rhizomes and you'll need to see the parts to divide them effectively. Dig them up and *hose off the soil* before dividing them.

Clump-forming Plants with Strap-like foliage

1. Lift established specimen (or, if potted, remove from pot).
2. Pull, cut, or hack apart the clump, ensuring each piece has its own roots, and replant into good soil or new pots.

Clump-forming Herbaceous Perennials

1. Lift clump.
2. Gently pull side shoots or plantlets from main plant and place into fresh soil.

Propagating Plants from Seed

Seed is by far the most cost- and time-efficient way of propagating large numbers of plants. For a beginner, the trick is to identify which plants are easily propagated from seed (see boxes on pp. 32 and 33). It's also important to know which plants will 'breed true' from seed; that is, whether the seedlings will have the same characteristics as the parent plant.

Which Plants?

Vegetables

Many of the older varieties of vegetables breed true from seed. Avoid collecting seed from those labelled F_1 hybrids; these are a complex cross and the offspring from the seeds of F_1 fruits often have quite different characteristics from the parent plants. However, classics and Heirloom varieties are easily raised from seed and you should not need to buy more seed after your initial year of growing them. Get lists and seeds from mail-order Seed Savers' Networks and organisations that specialise in preserving old-fashioned and true-breeding cultivars.

Fruit and Nut Trees

Many people raise stone and pome fruit (like apricots, cherries, apples and peaches), nuts and other trees from seed of grafted cultivars, but this is a risky business because there's no guarantee that the resulting tree will produce quality or quantity of fruit. Hence you could be waiting five years for a seedling to reach fruiting size only to discover that the few fruit it does produce have the taste and consistency of marbles dipped in vinegar. Alternatively, the fruit may be okay, but the tree will always lack vigour because of a poor root system (especially when the seed is from a grafted cultivar). Better in these cases to buy a grafted cultivar bare-rooted in winter from a reputable nursery (see p. 25). If you buy locally, you can be reasonably sure that the tree will thrive in your area, and that the rootstock onto which it has been grafted is suited to the local soil and climatic conditions.

Beginners often grow avocados from seed, but you run the risk of a tree which produces poor-quality fruit no matter how much fertiliser and water you provide. Of course, nature's dice could present you with a beauty, but the odds are against you.

Kiwi fruit, date palms and some pawpaws may be male or female; in this case, growing from seed means that not only may the fruit be of poor quality, but if the plant is male, you may get no fruit at all, even after twenty years!

Experienced gardeners with plenty of space and time can, of course, experiment with growing fruit and nut trees, but I believe that for those trying to save money it's false economy to skimp. It will be cheapest in the long run to buy quality cultivars from a reputable nursery.

Annuals and Biennials

As a general rule of thumb, those plants that are widely available from nurseries and garden centres germinate and grow easily from seed. Seed of the more common annuals is usually quite cheap to buy, especially when you consider the number of plants you produce from one small packet. At the end of your first season it is then, of course, essential not to cut the spent blooms or to rip out the plants once they finish producing flowers, but to keep a close eye on the developing seed pods so that you can collect them as or before they open.

Many biennials grow easily from seed. Unlike annuals, which germinate, grow, bloom and set seed in one year or less, biennials flower in their second year before dying. The box below lists annuals and biennials that grow easily from seed without special treatment. Just collect, store, and plant them next season (see pp. 23–4).

Easy-to-propagate Annuals and Biennials from Seed

(see also Easy-to-propagate Culinary Herbs on p. 39 and Naturalising Annuals and Biennials on p. 66)

Althaea rosea (Hollyhock)
Bellis perennis (English Daisy)
Centaurea cyanus (Cornflower)
Cosmos bipinnatus (Cosmos)
Digitalis purpurea (Foxglove)
Eschscholzia californica (Californian Poppy)
Campanula medium (Canterbury Bell)
Helianthus annuus (Sunflower)
Rhodanthe anthemoides (Paper Daisy)
Iberis sempervirens (Candytuft)
Lobelia erinus (Lobelia)
Matthiola spp. (stock)
Oenothera biennis (Evening Primrose)
Papaver rhoeas (Shirley Poppy)
Salvia splendens (Scarlet Sage)
Viola × wittrockiana (Pansy)

Ornamental Shrubs and Trees

Many ornamental shrubs and trees grow easily from seed but there is no simple way for the beginner to tell which do, or which will breed true (though, as a general rule of thumb, highly bred cultivars like camellias are less likely to produce a seedling with the same characteristics as the true species). Of course, you might be quite happy to grow, say, camellia cultivars that don't breed true, and enjoy the anticipation of a surprise flower.

Seed from species, especially Australian natives, is more likely to breed true than seed from cultivars, but the trick here is that many Australian natives are more easily propagated from cutting than from seed, or require special treatment before they'll germinate (see pp. 34–5 on pre-treating seed).

If there's a particular feature like flower or foliage colour that you want in a plant, your safest option is to check with a horticulturalist *before* you propagate from seed. That way, you'll be sure the feature will be present in the seedlings. If not, you'll know you'll have to propagate vegetatively (e.g. by cutting or division).

Most plant encyclopaedias and references (see Appendix 1) provide not only cultural requirements but also propagation methods for each species, so look up any plants you're unsure of.

Perennials and Herbaceous Perennials

Some perennials are suited to propagation by seed, others are not, and for those that produce seedlings with a range of flower colours and patterns (e.g. hellebores, penstemon cultivars, aquilegias) the resulting range of flowers is a bonus rather than a disadvantage.

Collecting Seed

Commonsense applies when collecting seed. Collect seed when it is ripe, not green. You can usually tell when seed is ripe because the capsule gets dry and brittle (or, in fruit, soft

---

Easy-to-propagate Perennials from Seed

Chrysanthemum parthenium (Feverfew)

Erigeron karvinskianus (Seaside Daisy)

Gaillardia spp.

Geum 'Mrs Bradshaw', G. 'Lady Stratheden' (avens)

Helleborus corsicus, H. *orientalis* (winter roses)

Lavandula spp. (lavenders)

Lupinus spp. (lupins)

Papaver nudicaule (Iceland Poppy)

Tanacetum parthenium (Feverfew)

Penstemon spp. (penstemons)

Scabiosa spp. (Scabious)

Verbascum spp. (mulleins)

---

and squishy), and pod or seed is released easily. Slightly unripe seed may also be collected but usually can't be stored and needs to be sown immediately. Germination rates are also likely to be lower.

Collect from healthy plants (not obviously diseased or insect-infested), and if collecting vegetable seeds, collect from the best producer (not, as may be tempting, the first one to shoot prematurely to seed!). If possible, collect from higher on the plant, where soil and bacteria are less likely to have splashed up onto pod or foliage.

When collecting from plants whose seed pods ripen and open explosively, you can tie a paper bag around the branch just before ripening to catch the seed. Avoid plastic bags, which trap moisture and may prevent drying or promote fungal diseases.

Some Australian native plants carry their seed in woody capsules (e.g. eucalypts, hakeas, banksias). Place the capsules in a paper bag in a warm, dry, sunny spot until they open or, for faster results, in a low oven

Easy-to-propagate Australian Natives from Seed

Acacia spp. (wattles)*
Agonis flexuosa (Willow Myrtle)
Banksia spp. (banksias)**
Callistemon spp. (bottlebrushes)
Cassia spp. (cassias)*
Casuarina spp. (sheoaks)**
Chrysocephalum spp. (everlastings)
Eucalyptus spp. (eucalypts)**
Hakea spp. (hakeas)**
Hardenbergia violacea (Native
   Sarsaparilla)*
Isotoma axillaris
Kennedia spp.*
Leptospermum spp. (tea-tree)
Pultenaea spp. (bush peas)*
Rhodanthe spp. (paper daisies)
Viola betonicifolia

* scarification necessary (see p. 35)
** seed in woody capsules: heat in low oven to
   extract seed (see p. 34)

for several hours (see Easy-to-propagate Australian Natives from Seed above).

Seeds in fleshy fruits (e.g. tomatoes) may be macerated. Squish the ripe fruit in a container and cover with water for a day or two. Then pour into a fine sieve and use a high-pressure spray of water to wash away the flesh. Spread the seed on a tray or blotting paper and allow it to dry thoroughly before storing. Berries may be treated in the same way or, if small or less fleshy, can be dried whole.

Storing Seed

Seed should be as clean as possible before it is stored so remove as much chaff and capsule as you can. If necessary, you can dust lightly with insecticide powder before storing. Store seed in glass or plastic if it is very dry, or paper envelopes if they can be effectively sealed. All seed should be clearly labelled with the species name and the date of collection. Containers should be stored in a clean, dark, dry place not susceptible to extremes of temperature or temperature fluctuation. Most seed will remain viable for several years or longer, although viability drops off with increasing age.

Sowing Seed

Seed may be simply sown either in situ for hardy species or annuals, or into containers for transplanting later. As a general rule of thumb, large seed should be sown deeper than fine seed: 2.5 to 3.5 times the diameter of the seed.

Don't sow too thickly, because poor air circulation around crowded seedlings makes them susceptible to 'damping off' (a fungal disease that attacks the stem of the seedling). Although large seed may be sown individually, smaller seed may be evenly sprinkled over propagating medium, the surface of which has been firmed and levelled with a block and watered. The seed may then be covered to the appropriate depth and lightly watered with a fine spray to ensure soil is not washed away. Very fine seed may be mixed with sand to prevent overly dense sowing. A few plants (e.g. primulas) require light to germinate, and these should be sprinkled on the damp surface of a fine-textured seed-raising mix, firmed down with a block, and watered with a fine spray.

Pre-treating Seed

A number of plants, notably many Australian natives (e.g. cassias, acacias, quandongs), have evolved a thick, hard seedcoat to prevent desiccation in our arid climate. This lets them survive long dry spells, and prevents them from germinating in inappropriately light showers of rain that are insufficient to support seedling growth afterwards.

Certain Northern Hemisphere plants (crab-apples, cherries, conifers) and most alpine plants (e.g. gentians, Edelweiss, Flannel Flower) are adapted to growing in very cold climates. Should they germinate in late autumn (when much of the seed ripens), the emerging seedlings would be quickly killed off by the icy winter. Hence these plants require a cold period (close to freezing) to break their dormancy before they will germinate.

Without treatment, seeds with hard coats or those from cold climate s may take weeks, months or even years to germinate. With treatment, the seeds will germinate much more quickly and evenly. Treatment for hard seedcoats is called '**scarification**' and treatment for cold-climate seed is called '**stratification**'.

Finally, the seeds of certain plants have complex combinations of physical *and* chemical germination inhibitors (e.g. eremophilas, thryptomenes, quandongs and boronias). Such seeds may require soaking in running water, storage in a dark place, and/or hormone treatment before they'll germinate, and are a challenge to the experts as well as beginners. Unless you're interested in experimenting, I'd advise against trying seed of these toughies. Luckily, most of them can be propagated by cuttings (see below).

Good reference books provide propagation as well as cultivation requirements, so you can identify the best techniques for your plant before you begin (see Appendix 1).

Scarification

Scarification is a treatment that breaks through the hard seedcoat, allowing water to enter so that the embryo can develop and germinate. You may scarify seed by using any of the following techniques:

1. Place the seeds in a container and pour over boiling water to just cover the seeds. Within twelve to twenty-four hours, most of the seeds should have swollen, indicating that the embryo has absorbed water and that the germination process has begun.
2. Nick the seedcoat with a scalpel or sharp instrument. This is obviously suited to larger seed or when smaller numbers are being propagated. Be sure to nick the seed at a smooth, unmarked spot, away from the point at which the roots emerge, to avoid damaging the embryo.
3. Rub the seed between sheets of medium to coarse sandpaper (depending on the thickness of the seedcoat). Once again, do not overabrade.
4. Certain seeds, especially those that are adapted to passing through the digestive tracts of animals, may benefit from soaking in a dilute acid solution, but these are exceptions. Check with your local Society for Growing Australian Plants (SGAP) branch for dilution rates if you plan to grow these plants.

Stratification

Place seeds that need stratification in the refrigerator for three to twelve weeks. Those which require moist stratification should be placed in damp propagating mix, peat or sphagnum, or sown into punnets before refrigeration. If you're not sure whether a plant you wish to propagate requires stratification or not, check in a good reference text (see Appendix 1).

Propagating Plants from Cuttings

Although successfully propagating plants by cuttings (or 'slips') requires a little more knowledge than you need for seed or division, many, many plants grow very easily using this technique, and are forgiving of mistakes.

Cuttings are basically pieces of plant, usually stems (with or without leaves attached, depending on the type of cutting), trimmed and inserted into propagating mix where, after a varying length of time (from weeks to months), they form roots.

Many different kinds of cuttings produce new plants from old: root cuttings, leaf cuttings, nodal cuttings, plus numerous variations on the theme. Most, however, fall into two broad categories: **softwood cuttings** and **hardwood cuttings**.

Softwood cuttings are taken during the growing season, and have leaves that use sunlight to photosynthesise and provide the energy to grow roots.

Hardwood cuttings are taken from deciduous plants during their dormant season. They are without leaves, and rely on stored energy in the stems to grow roots. For good books on growing more unusual types of cuttings, see Appendix 1.

Softwood (Leafy) Cuttings

When to Take
Late spring and early summer are ideal times to take softwood (leafy) cuttings in temperate areas. The soil has warmed and active growth has commenced, but the scorching heat of summer hasn't yet arrived. If you own a shadehouse, sheltered spot or live in a cooler region, you'll be able to propagate right through summer too, because the cuttings won't wilt.

Many exotics also strike in autumn before the soil becomes cold, but most native plants strike best in early summer once new growth has begun to harden.

Collecting Cutting Material
Always choose fresh, disease-free material, and work in a cool, sheltered spot. With the nails of your thumb and forefinger, pinch out any flower buds or blooms, so that none of the cutting's energy will be diverted from forming roots. If you need to store material for a day or two, wrap the stems in wet newspaper or place the bottoms of the stems in a bucket of water in a cool, shaded spot.

Making Cuttings
Tip cuttings (those taken from the very tip of a stem) strike easily unless very soft (floppy), in which case they're likely to wilt—you should then choose firmer material from further down the stem. Make each cutting 7–12 centimetres long, snipping just below a node (the point where a leaf emerges from a stem). Plants with more widely spaced nodes require longer cuttings. Trim the leaves from the lower two-thirds of the stem and dip the bottom centimetre into striking hormone only if you are propagating difficult or slow-to-strike material. Tap off the excess powder because too much can actually inhibit root formation.

Use a dibber or pencil to make planting holes, then insert the lower half to two-thirds of the cutting into small, individual tubes of cutting mix (see p. 28). Alternatively, place three to ten cuttings into each standard-sized pot and gently separate and repot when you see roots emerging from the drainage holes (new growth at the tip is often, but by no means always, a sign that the cutting has struck). This can take anything from two weeks to six months, so be patient!

If you're taking cuttings from further down the stem, make the top cut just above a node; otherwise the dimensions and treatment are as for tip cuttings.

Caring for Cuttings
Grow cuttings in a well-lit site protected from direct sun. Regular misting and watering will speed up rooting, but protect grey- or furry-leaved plants from overhead moisture and ensure air circulation is good because they're more susceptible to fungal attack.

Bottom heat speeds root formation on most cuttings but is not necessary for easy-to-strike plants (see p. 37).

Evergreen Cuttings
Evergreen cuttings are softwood cuttings of large or glossy-leaved species. They are usually taken in summer and, although not difficult to strike, may take many months to

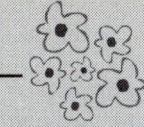

Easy-to-propagate Softwood Cuttings

Achillea spp. (yarrows)

Alogyne hueglii

Argyranthemum fruticosum (Marguerite Daisy)

Cheiranthus spp. (wallflowers)

Cistus spp. (rock roses)

Erigeron karvinskianus (Seaside Daisy)

Correa spp. (correas)

Fuchsia spp. (fuchsias)

Hebe spp. (hebes)

Helichrysum bracteatum (Strawflower)

Hedera helix (English Ivy)

Impatiens walleriana (Impatiens)

Pelargonium cultivars

Penstemon spp. (penstemons)

Phlomis fruticosa (Jerusalem Sage)

Polygonum capitatum

Tradescantia spp. (but avoid the invasive *T. fluminensis*)

form roots. Providing you can maintain humidity and moisture, you should have success with the easier ones such as *Clethra arborea*, viburnums and Sweet Bay.

Hardwood Cuttings

When to Take
Late autumn and winter in temperate climates are ideal times for propagating deciduous plants. This is because most deciduous plants have soft leaves that wilt very quickly and are therefore unsuited to softwood cuttings taken during the growing season. So hardwood cuttings are best made just after the leaves have fallen (leaf fall is your guide in warmer climates, too).

Collecting Cutting Material
Because these cuttings are without leaves they can't photosynthesise; instead, they

rely on food stored in the stems to form roots. For this reason, it's important to choose stems of at least pencil thickness if you can. Thinner stems also strike but are usually slower to get going.

Making Cuttings
Hardwood cuttings should have at least two, preferably three, nodes (the leaves have fallen but you can usually identify the nodes as ridges or bumps on the stem) and may be 10–30 centimetres long. Plants with nodes that are widely spaced, like glory vine and elderberry, will make longer cuttings than plants with nodes closer together, like forsythia or currants.

Use sharp secateurs and make the lower cut just below a node and the upper cut just above a node. Some growers like to angle the lower cut to more easily identify the bottom.

Make sure your cutting is not upside down (believe me, it happens!), insert the lower half to two-thirds into a free-draining propagating mix, or insert directly into good garden soil.

Caring for Cuttings
Place in an open position with good air circulation, and then repot or plant directly

Easy-to propage Hardwood Cuttings

Aloysia triphylla (Lemon Verbena)

Chaenomeles japonica (Flowering Quince)

Forsythia × *intermedia* (Common Forsythia)

Hibiscus syriacus

Hydrangea spp. and cultivars

Rosa spp. (especially older varieties that thrive on their own roots)

Sambucus nigra (Elderberry)

Vitis coignetiae (Crimson Glory Vine)

Ribes spp. (currants)

into final position in early spring when struck, just before buds burst, taking care not to damage the roots. Water your new plant conscientiously during its first season.

Propagating Bulbs, Corms and Tubers

Bulbous plants are terrifically easy to propagate and you can eventually grow many plants from a single bulb, corm or tuber. Most increase naturally by this method anyway, so all you're doing is giving nature a little hurry-along.

Bulbs, corms and tubers are specially modified buds, stems and underground stems/roots of plants respectively. They grow under the ground (some may protrude slightly above the soil), fed by above-ground photosynthesising leaves.

Bulbs

Each year, a single bulb usually increases by forming sidebulbs around it. These sidebulbs vary in size from very tiny to almost as large as the parent plant. A common, instantly recognisable bulb is garlic, and division of garden bulbs is as easy as (and identical to) separating a clove from the knob.

Deciduous bulbs like daffodils and nerines can be dug once the leaves have died down. For the best results, you should *always* wait until the above-ground foliage has yellowed and died off before propagating herbaceous bulbs, because this allows the nutrients in the leaves to be transported and stored in the bulb, allowing for stronger growth and better flowers next season. Separate the sidebulbs and store in a cool, dark, dry place until next season, or plant immediately into the ground.

Evergreen bulbs can be divided at any time, though it's best to avoid very hot weather to minimise wilting.

Easy-to-propagate Bulbs

Amaryllis belladonna (Belladonna Lily)
Hyacinthoides hispanica (Spanish Bluebell)
Iris tingitana × I. xiphium (Dutch Iris)
Lachenalia aloides 'Quadricolor' (Soldier Boys)
Leucojum aestivum (Snowflake)
Lilium longiflorum (Christmas Lily)
Muscari armeniacum (Grape Hyacinth)
Narcissus spp. (jonquils)
Nerine bowdenii (Nerine)
Sprekelia formosissima (Jacobean Lily)
Tulipa spp. (tulips)

Scaly bulbs, such as liliums, are scaly in appearance, resembling an artichoke rather than an onion. They form sidebulbs that can be divided: you may need to use a sharp knife to separate them. Scaly bulbs can also be propagated by removing the largest scales, ensuring there's a piece of the woody base of the bulb attached. These scales take time to grow big enough to flower, but you can get a dozen or more new plants from a single bulb. Many liliums also form bulbils in the leaf axils up the stem. These bulbils resemble small, shiny seeds and can be planted to form new plants.

Corms

Corms include gladioli and watsonia and are specially modified plant stems. Most readily form cormlets around the bottom edge of the parent corm, and these separate easily, falling away by themselves when you dig the corm (but take care, because cormlets can be very tiny and easy to miss. As for bulbs, you should wait until the foliage has fully died down before digging corms.

Easy-to-propagate Corms

Babiana stricta (Baboon Flower)
Crocosmia cultivars (Montbretia)
Dierama pulcherrimum (Fairy Fishing Rods)
Freesia cultivars (freesias)
Gladiolus spp. (gladioli)
Ixia spp. (ixias)
Watsonia borbonica (Watsonia)

Tubers

Tubers include dahlias, Dracunculus and Oxalis. Potatoes are the most commonly known tuber in Australia, and it's possible to propagate most tubers by cutting them into pieces as you would potatoes, ensuring each piece has an 'eye' from which the new plant will grow. Certain tubers (e.g. tree dahlias) only have one growing point at the end of the tuber, or several that are clustered closely together at the stem end. In this case, each tuber grows a new plant, but you won't be able to divide each individual tuber.

Easy-to-propagate Tubers

Alstroemeria cultivars
Anemone pavonina (Peacock Anemone)
Dahlia cultivars
Dracunculus vulgaris
Gloriosa superba (Glory Lily)
Oxalis spp. (avoid invasive species)
Ranunculus asiaticus
Zantedeschia aethiopica (White Arum Lily)

Propagating Plants You Can Eat

You can save lots of money in the supermarket and greengrocer by propagating and growing you own kitchen herbs.

Easy-to-propagate Culinary Herbs

Anthriscus cerefolium (Chervil)—S
Allium sativum (Garlic)—D from organic stock
Allium schoenoprasum (Chives)—S D
Artemisia dracunculus (French Tarragon)—C D
Borago officinalis (Borage)—S
Coriandrum sativum (Coriander)—S
Cumimum cyminum (Cumin)—S
Cymbopogon citratus (Lemon Grass)—D
Eruca sativa (Rocket)—S
Foeniculum vulgare (Fennel)—S D
Levisticum officinale (Lovage)—S D
Melissa officinalis (Lemon balm)—S D C
Mentha spp. (mints)—C D
Nasturtium officinale (Watercress)—S D C
Ocimum basilicum (Basil)—S
Origanum vulgare (Oregano)—S D C
Petroselinum crispum (Parsley)—S
Trigonella foenum-graecum (Fenugreek)—S
Rosmarinus officinalis (Rosemary)—C
Salvia officinalis (Sage)—S C
Satureja spp. (savories)—S C
Thymus spp. (Thymes)—S D C

S = seed
C = cutting
D = division

CHAPTER 4

Tools and Equipment

Buying Tools

Tools and equipment are essential in the creation and maintenance of a garden, but you're unlikely to need as many of them as you might at first think. You do not—repeat *not*—need the ten-gear, low-noise, four-wheel-drive ride-on econo-mower with sunroof, electric windows and power steering as the advertising would have you believe. Get sucked into the bigger-is-better rat-race at your peril.

Still, I suggest several basic caveats. Buying cheap tools, especially tools that you're likely to use a lot, is false economy. One expensive but excellent pair of secateurs will last a lifetime (well, twenty years), while the local supermarket specials are likely to blunt and fall apart within a season. Calculate value for money: is that cheap pair truly one-twentieth the price of the quality pair? And even if it is, do you really want to revisit the shop to replace it every year? Providing you look after them (no leaving them out in the weather!), quality tools are a lifetime investment, a pleasure to use and safer to boot.

You can occasionally pick up good-quality second-hand tools at clearing sales, deceased estates and garage sales, but first become familiar with the prices of the same tools bought new, and check to see that the second-hand tools have been well cared for: metal parts may show a little surface rust but should not be heavily pocked or corroded, and wooden parts should be firm without splits or splinters. However, if the blade is particularly good, remember you can buy replacement handles for most larger tools (axes, rakes, spades, picks and so on).

Of course, while you usually get what you pay for with precision tools like secateurs, the home-brand variety of kitchen knives (for weeding) is as effective as the silver-plate. A bucket is a bucket. And a locally made product may be better quality in dollar-for-dollar terms than an English import with a huge duty whacked onto the price.

Beware those gimmicky products sold at garden shows or expos. The spruiker is usually very good, unlike the product (if it's so fantastic, why isn't it available in every garden shop?).

Before you buy anything, prioritise your needs. There's a basic must-have list for every gardener, but many tools are a bit like those mysterious settings on your microwave or video that you know are there but never bother to use. Also, you may need certain tools (such as a pick and a crowbar) during the establishment phase of a garden but have less use for them later.

1. The Essential Tool List

New gardeners may be tempted to rush to the garden or hardware store and buy every tool on offer. Avoid the temptation. Tools, especially large ones (and plenty of the small ones as well), are pricey, and I've already explained why cheap tools are expensive in the long run. If you buy all the tools advertised in catalogues and gardening magazines, you'll have no money left for the garden proper! So how do you determine what you really need?

Your basic list of must-haves varies depending on your garden and on you, of course. There's no point in buying a mower if you have no lawn; nor should you buy a pick if you have serious lower back problems. Will you be moving a lot of soil? Pruning lots of trees and shrubs? When? (There's no point in buying electric hedgeclippers and an electric mulcher the moment you move to a bare block, but not so silly if you inherit a well-established and rather overgrown garden you need to whip into shape). Still, it's possible to narrow the field considerably.

These items are on my list. Adapt to your own needs depending on your site.

spade	bucket
rake	wheelbarrow
leaf rake	hose(s)
pick	sprinkler(s)
weeding knife	lawn mower
hand trowel	hedgeclippers
secateurs	spray unit
watering can	

There. That's it. A maximum of fifteen tools on the 'essential' list for the most serious of gardeners. The remaining items are useful, desirable, but not essential—it's almost always possible to borrow or hire this equipment. A pruning saw is nice, but an ordinary saw substitutes just fine when money is tight.

1. Spade

In my opinion, a spade is first on the list. Buy the best quality you can afford. A good spade will double as a **shovel** when shifting gravel, but a shovel won't double as a spade when digging because it slices into the soil less effectively. In fact, I find shovels hold too much gravel or soil for comfortable use, but you may disagree on both counts—it depends on your physique and technique. Still, I recommend that you don't buy a spade and shovel simultaneously; instead, wait a while to see whether the spade is enough for your needs.

A good sharp spade can also be used as a **lawn edger** and is cheaper than a **whipper-snipper**.

I also find myself using a spade in almost all cases where conventional gardening books recommend the use of a **fork**, though I do own a good one. I lift perennials and dig beds with the spade, perhaps because my own garden soil is on the heavy side. The only times I find the fork particularly useful is when I'm moving light, fibrous or coarse compost (but even then I've used a spade by sliding the blade in at soil level from the side of the heap), and for using the flat of the tines to break up cloddy soil. Once again, there's little doubt you'll find a fork practical, but hold off on buying one until you're sure the purchase cost warrants the use.

You shouldn't need a **trenching spade** unless you're planning on installing one heck of a lot of agricultural pipe or irrigation hose, or if you're going into the landscaping business.

And, with the exception of gardeners who own acreages, if you're thinking of buying a **rotary hoe** you don't need to read this book. It's elbow grease for the rest of us, I'm afraid.

2. Pick

A pick is high on my list because my partner and I moved into a house on a sloping block with lots of clay banks that had to be recontoured. The spade just didn't cut it (pardon me). On the other hand, there's little point (sorry) in buying a pick if you live on a sand dune or lack the stamina needed for its use. Nor are you likely to need a pick if you're working a well-established garden with good soil, or a small inner-city block.

The double-ended variety, with a pick at one end and a **mattock** (a forged blade) at the other, is the most versatile. A mattock is unbeatable for breaking up hard clods of soil, a bit like a heavy-duty hoe.

Buy the heaviest one you can comfortably handle (when you use a pick correctly, its own weight and a lever action does much of the work).

3. Rake and Leaf Rake

I'm afraid rakes and leaf rakes are not inter-changeable—you'll need both. A leaf rake is light and relatively cheap (you can pick up a good one for $15–20). It's worth spending a little extra because the more expensive ones are slightly wider (translating to significantly less raking time), and the tines last longer with less distortion. Some gardeners I know swear by the metal leaf rakes, but I find that they distort more quickly (but then, I often find myself raking up stones, twigs and the odd clod of soil with the leaves, so their poor track record with me may be due to misuse rather than to a lack of quality).

If you want to save money, the price of a leaf rake is small potatoes indeed when com-pared with one of those special outdoor vacuum cleaners or—my pet hate—**leaf-blowers** (in any case, no one serious about saving money would buy one of these, because you can't blow leaves onto your compost heap; instead, I have a nasty suspi-cion that many environmentally unaware gardeners use these blowers to move their leaves to footpaths and gutters, adding pollu-tants to stormwater drains).

A good leaf rake does almost as good a job as a garden **broom**, though gardeners more fastidious than me will want the latter for driveways and entertaining areas (in this dry continent where water is such a precious resource, you'd never hose your driveway, would you?). Your ordinary household broom should be sufficient for porches and paving around the house unless these areas get par-ticularly muddy.

An ordinary rake is essential for smooth-ing garden beds and spreading mulch. Once again, don't skimp on quality. Make sure that the handle is the right length for you—short ones get you in the lower back.

4. Crowbar

A crowbar is one of those awkward tools. You're unlikely to use it often, but when you do need one, there is no substitute. Consider a crowbar if you'll be doing a lot of structural work—fences, retaining walls, pergolas, or carports. **Hole augers** also save hours, espe-cially when used in combination with a crowbar when digging holes for posts. Both augers and crowbars are ideal tools to borrow rather than buy. Once again, be guided by what you plan to do in your garden.

5. Secateurs

All serious gardeners should have a pair of good secateurs. Buy left-handed ones if, like me, you're a southpaw.

6. Weeding Knife

My favourite weeding knife is, in fact, a plas-terer's knife (see also p. 67). Its short handle and blade are easier to wield than those of the classic two-pronged **weeding fork**, and it's also ideal for loosening soil around plants with a slicing motion, like a mini-hoe. You can buy plasterer's knives from hardware stores for $10–15.

Broad, flat-bladed bread-and-butter knives are okay too, but I find the blade is a little long, narrow and flexible for heavy soil. Of course, I know gardeners who swear by these old table knives. Choose what suits you.

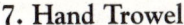

7. Hand Trowel

Hand trowels are useful, depending on the kind of gardening you're doing. Though I use mine only occasionally, I've included it on the essential list because I know so many gardeners who can't do without them. Hand trowels are ideal for planting seedlings and annuals, and for loosening soil, but a little heavy and clumsy for most weeding jobs.

If you need one, spend big on a hand trowel with a strong, inflexible shaft and moulded handle. A cheap one will last one afternoon.

I've never bothered with a multi-pronged **hand fork** but, once again, you might feel differently.

8. Bucket

Wash the bucket after use and you'll be able to use it in the laundry as well, but for the price of a few dollars you may as well buy two. Keep one bucket specifically for mixing herbicides (see p. 68–9).

9. Watering Can

You can buy metal or plastic. Personally, I find the plastic ones more durable, but that's because I leave cans standing around with a bit of water in them—the metal ones rust and the tiny flakes block the spray rose. Whichever you buy, choose one with a removable rose (there will be times when you want to pour, rather than sprinkle).

10. Wheelbarrow

Buy a wheelbarrow if you'll be moving a lot of soil, compost, gravel, or weeds around the garden; if you can afford one, choose a builder's barrow. Check dimensions and try out the barrow before you buy, especially if you're a short person.

Those large garden sheets with drawstring or handles around the edges are great for light compost and small loads, but not much chop for anything else.

11. Hose(s)

Buy one, unless you're prepared to cart a helluva lot of buckets. Heavy-duty non-kink ones last longer, unless you own a puppy, in which case buy the cheapest hose you can find. You'll have to replace it soon, anyway.

12. Sprinkler

You'll need one even if you've installed an irrigation system. Even the best irrigation system leaves dry spots, and you'll have plants that need an extra drink between the main program. For the purpose of top-up watering I'd recommend a butterfly-head sprinkler mounted on a stake. Alternatively, you can buy a special kind of stake that is designed to grip the ordinary adjustable **spray nozzle** you attach to the end of a hose. This option is cheap and versatile if you need a spray nozzle attachment on your hose. I don't. I rarely use spray nozzles and, in fact, often remove them before hand watering—I regulate the spray from a hose more quickly and effectively with my forefinger placed against the end.

See Chapter 8 for more tips on irrigation.

13. Lawn Mower

Unless you want to pay a mowing service, you'll need a mower if you have a lawn (see p. 66 for dense groundcover plants that make good lawn substitutes). Don't overlook cylinder or reel mowers. They're very cheap, give a neat cut, require little maintenance and no fuel except your muscle power, and don't break down. Plus you get fit using them.

Ride-on mowers are only for gardeners with acreages. A cheap alternative for gardeners with acreages are the four-legged varieties of mower (Baa and Billy G are excellent brands).

14. Hedgeclippers

I recommend muscle-powered hedgeclippers, not electric ones (the latter are much more expensive, and in my opinion are worth buying only if you have something like an established cypress hedge to maintain).

Like microwave ovens, hedgeclippers are one of those tools you buy and immediately wonder how you ever managed without. I use my hedgeclippers for tasks that I previously did laboriously with secateurs—notably, pruning of shrubs is now done in a fraction of the time. I also use my hedgeclippers in the place of a **lawntrimmer** or a **whippersnipper** for neatening rank lawn in areas the mower can't reach.

Buy the best quality you can afford. Look for rubber stoppers between the handles, which cushion the impact of closing blades and save on wrist soreness. If you're no Arnold Schwarzenegger, remember that longer handles provide more leverage.

15. Spray Unit
You'll need a proper unit if you're into large-scale pest control, although if you're only using tiny amounts of pesticide you can buy a little hand-held sprayer. Otherwise, buy a good-quality unit. Watch out for cheap ones that disintegrate in UV radiation. Maintain them thoroughly.

TIP

Disabled Gardeners
A quick mention here of special tools and equipment for disabled gardeners. These are available for purchase and/or hire from certain chemists, Independent Living Centres and hardware stores. Particularly useful are kneelers, which help you rise from a kneeling position, and hand tools with special grips for arthritis sufferers. Ergonomic spades also make a big difference for gardeners with back problems.

---

2. The 'Nice-to-have-but-not-essential' Tool List

These tools are convenient, but their tasks can be performed by tools on the 'essential' list. Buy them only if you've some cash to spare, if you have a great deal of ongoing work that requires the more specialised tool, or if you find yourself wishing you owned the real McCoy every time you have to use the alternative.

broom	lawn edger
chainsaw	leaf blower/vacuum
crowbar	mattock
fork	mulcher
garden sheet	pruning saw
hand fork	rotary hoe
hoe (Dutch, single,	shovel
swan-necked or	spray nozzles (for hose)
double-bladed)	trailer
hole auger	trenching spade
ladder	whippersnipper

Alternatives to Buying

In many cases, buying is not the best option. This applies especially to very expensive equipment and to tools that you use once only or rarely. Choose from the following options.

Borrowing

Be courteous. Return the item promptly, clean and in good condition. If you find yourself borrowing the tool every weekend, this is a message that you need your own: you *should* buy one or risk losing the friendship of the lender. Return chainsaws sharp and with a can of petrol. Ditto mulchers.

Weddings, Birthdays and Special Events

Garden tools are the perfect wedding gift for couples just moving into their first home. If you're in this situation, put them on your list and hope to receive something a bit more useful than five toasters.

Joint Purchase

This option can be enormously cost-effective but is also fraught with danger. More than one family feud has begun with squabbles about who's responsible for servicing the mulcher, and the location of the trailer. Still, if you have a close, established relationship with a relative, friend, or neighbour, consider buying expensive tools jointly. Check out the legal ramifications first, if you wish; certainly you should determine some ground rules (e.g. who has the item, when, and for how long; where the item is to be stored, and how maintenance is to be paid for). This kind of cooperative agreement is ideal for expensive items that are important but that are used rarely and spend most of their time hibernating in the tool shed. Mulchers, trailers, chainsaws and possibly mowers are suitable for shared ownership.

Cheap Alternatives and Multipurpose Tools

These were touched on in the list of essential tools. Hedgeclippers double as secateurs and lawn edgers, hand mowers are cheaper than powered ones, spades may be used as shovels and lawn edgers, and so on.

Hiring

For expensive items or those that are a hassle to store or maintain, this is a good option. Once again, trailers, chainsaws, and mulchers are good candidates. If the fee is a 24-hour one and you need the tool for only a morning, check whether one of your neighbours wants to share in the hire costs (but beware: because *your* name is on the hire contract, *you're* responsible for returning the item in good condition). If you find yourself hiring an item regularly, it's probably more cost-effective to buy one.

CHAPTER 5

Landscaping Materials

Unless you own a balcony or courtyard, landscaping materials will most likely be the biggest initial expense you incur in establishing a new garden. Existing gardens are cheaper because the framework of paving, lawns, soil, retaining walls, concrete, and fencing are already in place, and you can modify the garden gradually if you wish. A new garden, on the other hand, generally needs lots of imports. There's your house sitting in the middle of a bombsite, surrounded by piles of building rubble. If you're lucky and the builders have retained some, there will be mountains of topsoil too. Still, the old rule of careful planning applies: better to wait a few months and be sure of what you want rather than buying-up big on pavers only to discover that concrete would have been better.

Principles of Smart Buying

Calculate Carefully
Check and double-check those figures when working out volumes of soil, areas of paving bricks, or lengths of sleepers for walls. Undercalculating will incur an additional cost because you'll need to pay a second delivery fee. Overcalculating will leave you with a pile of bricks or soil, though in the case of bricks and pavers, this is not always such a bad thing because they can be stacked neatly down the back of the yard and used in years to come—you'd be surprised how many ways they come in handy.

Double-check with the Supplier
When you order your materials, run the numbers past the supplier: 'I'm paving an area nine metres by three in a herringbone pattern: how many bricks do you think I'll need?' Don't be surprised if the supplier quotes you a slightly higher number than you've calculated: they're not being greedy, but are factoring in things like damaged bricks, bricks that need to be cut and so on.

Shop Around
You should shop around for the best price. Get a few quotes; you'll soon have an idea of the figures. The more money involved, the more phone calls you should make. Get several quotes and don't forget to factor in delivery costs: a load of cheap soil from the other side of town may well end up more expensive than the local supplier whose soil is dearer but whose delivery costs are lower. If you choose a local supplier, it's worth making them your first port of call consistently: as a regular customer you may be able to negotiate discounts.

46

Buying in Bulk

Buying in bulk almost always minimises delivery costs, so aim for one big load rather than two smaller ones. If you wish to pave two areas, it's generally better to save up and buy enough bricks for both areas, rather than doing each one separately and doubling delivery costs. However, there are exceptions. Check prices, because some suppliers use a large (expensive) truck for big loads, and a smaller (cheaper) one for small loads. If your volume only just warrants the large truck and most of its capacity is not being used, you'll be better off getting two loads in the smaller truck.

Hiring a Trailer

Alternatively, if you're prepared to do the work yourself, you can save money by hiring a trailer. Daily rates are reasonable but make sure you have enough loads to warrant the fee and enough stamina to last the day shovelling! Remember to plan carefully so you have room to unload your loads of soil, gravel or sleepers; take advantage of return trips by dropping a few loads of household rubbish at the dump. Most friends are happy to lend you their trailer, but observe the basic courtesies and return it clean, on time, and (depending on the tastes of your friends) accompanied by a bunch of flowers, box of chocolates or bottle of wine.

If you're on good terms with your neighbours, you may be able to share delivery or trailer-hire costs. Arrange to use the trailer for half a day each, or get a single delivery dropped at one house and help with the barrowing.

Seasonal Variations

Some landscaping suppliers are hectic in spring and summer, and quieter during winter. You may be able to take advantage of these seasonal variations and negotiate cheaper rates, especially if you're buying a lot.

Cash Discounts

Remember that every time you buy with a credit card, the seller must pay a portion of the money (about 3 per cent) to the bank (this is in addition to the interest the bank receives from the buyer).

Consider negotiating for a cash discount whenever possible. You'll end up in front and the seller doesn't lose. Of course the banks *do* lose, so if you feel sorry for them then by all means use your credit card.

Cheap Sources and Alternatives to Buying

Unless you're one of those lucky and necessarily rich people who like to buy only top-of-the-range and brand-new, you'll be able to save lots of money by going second-hand and by scrounging. Often, it'll be a case of grabbing opportunities. You see a stack of pots next to your friend's garbage bin. If the pots are, in fact, destined for the dump, your friend will almost certainly be more than happy to chuck them your way instead. Of course, there's a danger in being overzealous. If you don't want your friends to hide their possessions when they know you're coming, don't be too greedy! A simple request ('If you're buying some plants could you please hang onto the pots for me?') made once should be enough. So, where can you go for what?

Bricks

Bricks for paving can be bought from demolition sites (often at auction—check the newspaper). There are also yards that specialise in reselling second-hand bricks (look in the *Yellow Pages*). These bricks are cheaper than new ones (and also cheaper than new pavers), but you'll still need several hundred dollars for a modest driveway. You can reduce the cost considerably by buying uncleaned bricks, but think carefully before you choose this option. By the time you're chipping the mortar from the fourth side of the thousandth brick, your fingers blistered and abraded from days of tedious chiselling, it's likely that you'll be heartily regretting your choice. Believe me.

> ### TIP
> **Stone, rock, brick, timber and logs** are usually expensive when bought from the garden centre. Shop around and remember that it's often better to go direct to the source.

Logs

Logs are excellent for edging garden beds in informal gardens, but untreated logs lying on the ground will rot away within five to ten years depending on their diameter and the durability of the wood. This is okay if you're getting logs free (e.g. from tree-lopping), but not so good if you're buying them.

Log rounds for stepping stones are popular too, though personally I can't understand why. Bought from garden centres they're expensive and don't last long. Worse, they become dangerously slippery in damp conditions. When buying, check value for money, shop around at different garden centres and nurseries, and decide whether a few slabs of slate or pavers might not be cheaper in the long run.

Mulches and Composts

Mulches and composts are essential components of a healthy garden. Both play a key role in soil fertility, promoting lush growth, suppressing weeds and retaining soil moisture. See pp. 75–9 for more details, including how to make your own compost.

If your own garden is new and generates little compost or mulch, don't despair. If you have access to a trailer, or even a few bags and the boot of a car, you can find very cheap composts and mulches.

Baled Straw
Try your local feed merchant or farmers' co-op rather than garden centre for a better price on

Buying Cheaper Plants

After one season in the garden the tube (front) and pot (rear) specimens will be of similar size. Buy tube-stock instead of standard-sized pots for a cost saving of 30 to 55 per cent.

Pot-bound plants like this agapanthus may lack vigour while still in their pots but are great bargains when on the 'sales' table. Remove from the pot, tease out the roots, or lightly cut the rootball with a knife before planting into the garden.

You can easily divide potted plants such as sage (left) and thyme (right). Choose full pots, upend, then slice down through the rootball as if you were slicing a birthday cake. You'll end up with two, four, six or more plants.

When buying seedlings, consider the price of the container and the number of seedlings. Here, a generous pot of coriander seedlings (left) and marjoram (right).

Separate seedlings into individual plants, pairs, or small clumps. The pot of coriander yielded about 100 individual plants; the pot of marjoram yielded about 35 plants—excellent value for money. Plant separated seedlings and give TLC during establishment.

When buying seedlings, bigger is not necessarily better. Here, the younger and smaller Lobelia seedlings on the left are healthier than those on the right, which, because they have been in the punnet for longer and have depleted the nutrients in the mix, are 'leggy' and not growing well.

Hardwood Cuttings

The spacing of nodes on hardwood cuttings varies. In all cases the lower cut (the end to go into the soil) is made immediately below a node. To prevent underground suckering you can rub buds off the lower two-thirds of hardwood cuttings.

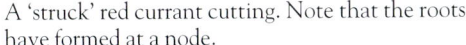

A 'struck' red currant cutting. Note that the roots have formed at a node.

Softwood Cuttings

Collect healthy, lush, disease-free growth for softwood cuttings. Trim cuttings, removing the lower two-thirds of leaf from the stem of each. These tip cuttings are ready to plant into propagating mix.

Use a dibber to make holes in the mix, insert cuttings, firm down the mix and water well. Cover the cuttings with a clear plastic bag (snip corners to allow ventilation) supported by bent wires that have been inserted into the pot.

Dividing Clump-forming Perennials with Strap-like Leaves

Lift the clump with a fork (or remove from pot) and separate into pieces (you'll be able to pull apart amenable species with your hands but you'll need a knife, axe, spade or hacksaw for plants with tough, woody rhizomes).

Trim excess leaf growth before replanting.

Propagating Bulbs, Corms and Tubers

Most bulbs form side bulbs after a season. Simply dig up the bulbs, pull side bulbs from the original, and replant.

Scaly bulbs, such as these liliums, may be propagated by removing the scales and planting them shallowly into a well-drained mix. Each scale will grow into a new bulb.

Corms like this gladiolus usually form cormlets around the base and sides of the original. Remove the cormlets and replant for each to grow into a new plant.

Some bulbs form 'bulbils' in the leaf axils. Each bulbil looks like a seed. Remove and plant these tiny bulbils so the top is just at soil level, and each bulbil will grow into a new plant.

Some tubers produce eyes, or buds, only at their top end. The tubers are the swollen lower sections, and the sprouting buds are the purplish and whitish shoots near the centre. When separating these tubers, make sure each piece has a shoot or bud as well as tuber.

baled straw. 'Spoiled' hay is bad for animals but perfect for gardens as a weed-suppressing mulch that's already begun to break down.

Compost

Many local rubbish dumps now direct organic/garden waste to particular areas, compost them, and then resell at very cheap rates. This is good value, with the odd boot or two (and weed seeds) thrown in free.

Lawn Clippings

Ask friends and neighbours for lawn clippings. Commercial lawn-mowing franchises and businesses are often more than happy to get rid of loads (they otherwise have to pay to take them to the local dump). Make sure you have plenty of space, because after you've rung the contractor and offered your front garden as a drop-off place, you may get more clippings than you bargained for! Compost some (mix it with coarser materials so it doesn't become a smelly anaerobic sludge) and use the rest as mulch. Don't spread fresh lawn clippings too thickly, especially in damp conditions, or they'll mat and be stubborn to break down; and don't pile them up against the stems of trees or shrubs because the heat and moisture of the decaying blades can cause collar rot.

Leaf and Wood Mulch

Tree-loppers, often those employed by local councils, will drop a truckload of leaf and wood mulch on your driveway for a small or no fee. Contact your local council for details. Leave the mulch piled in a heap for a few months to create rich compost, or spread thickly on garden beds for a natural-looking, aesthetically attractive mulch.

Pine Needles

Some forestry departments will let you take a trailer or two of pine needles. Check with the ranger first, because you may need a permit (in South Australia at time of writing, both permits and pine needles are free). Acidic pine needles are long-lasting and excellent for alkaline soils (see Tip on p. 62) or for mulching acid-loving plants like currants, blueberries and strawberries. Pine needles also contain chemicals that inhibit seed germination, so are excellent for suppressing weeds.

Sawdust

Many furniture manufacturers and joiners are happy for you to collect their rubbish—just watch out for nails. Some sawmills sell sawdust very cheaply or give it away. Just back your trailer under a hopper and it is filled in a minute or two. Sawdust makes a particularly good, long-lasting, weed-suppressing mulch for paths. Alternatively, mix it with poultry manure or high-nitrogen chemical fertilisers for a rich, soft, crumbly compost.

Seaweed

Collect it yourself, but remember to check local council regulations and Coastal Protection Authority restrictions (some prohibit the collection of seaweed from beaches). Rinse the seaweed first to remove excess salt, then use it as a mulch.

Pavers

You can buy 'seconds' pavers—that is, new pavers that have cracked, warped or chipped during manufacture. They are very cheap, but beware. Check the quality of the seconds very carefully (are they perhaps 'thirds', or even 'fourths'?). An acquaintance availed himself of this so-called 'bargain' only to find that more than half the pavers on the pallet were so bad they were unusable. Not only that, but the ones he did lay had to be pulled up a year later because the uneven result just got worse with seasonal soil moisture fluctuations. In other words, a complete waste of money.

Pots and Containers

New

Terracotta pots look lovely but are hugely expensive. Imitation ones of plastic are cheaper but not cheap, and the good old black plastic tubs and pots are still the best value for money. If you're buying new pots, avoid ones in white or fancy colours: black pots last longer than any other colour because they're the most UV stable.

If you need a large number of big containers for growing (say) trees, bags are cheap alternatives. Black plastic bags aren't as durable as tubs and are difficult to re-use (they tend to tear when you take out the plant), but they'll last for several years before you plant your tree into the ground.

Second-hand

Although you should *always* wash any second-hand pots from any source to avoid importing diseases or weed seeds into your garden, second-hand containers are a great way of saving money.

The local **rubbish dump** is an excellent source of second-hand pots. They'll be cheap (or even free) and you'll definitely get bargains. **Garage sales** are also good. Be flexible and open to possibilities: remember that

almost any strong, non-perishable container with drainage holes (you can drill these yourself) can be filled with soil and used to house plants. Below (see Tip) are some ideas to get you started.

Many **nurseries** will be happy to sell you old pots, especially non-standard sizes and styles (but then, you won't be looking into the mouths of any horses, will you?) and especially if you're a regular customer. You'll probably need to go around the back of the shed and collect the pots yourself.

Nursery suppliers supply pots, soil and miscellany to retail nurseries. Most nursery suppliers are wholesale only, but you can check in the *Yellow Pages* for those that also

---

> ## TIP
>
>
>
> ### Hard Rubbish
> Many councils specify 'hard rubbish' collection days, when residents place on the footpath all kinds of useful things (like pots) for collection by the rubbish removal contractor. If you're driving past and see something you like, you **must get permission from the resident who is discarding the hard refuse** *before* **you take it away. If you don't get permission first, the council and/or contractor can prosecute you for theft.**

> ## TIP
>
> ### Containers for Growing Plants
> Here are some ideas to get you started. Remember that you may need to drill extra drainage holes.
> - buckets
> - large-diameter terracotta drainage pipes or old chimney pots (seal one end with wire mesh, old weedmat or shadecloth)
> - margarine/ice-cream containers
> - old laundry sinks, lavatories and bath tubs (great for water plants)
> - old rubbish bins (plastic, wire mesh, steel)
> - old wheelbarrows (or just the barrow part)
> - polystyrene cups
> - polystyrene/foam vegetable boxes (excellent for seeds and cuttings)
> - troughs
> - tyres (stacked two to three high for larger plants)
> - washing-machine innards
> - watering cans

retail. Retail suppliers will sell pots and tubes in bulk (boxes of 250, 500 or 1000), and these numbers are usually well beyond the needs of the average home gardener. Still, if you're keen to buy new, consider finding a few like-minded gardeners to share the costs. Propagation nurseries may sell you second-hand tubes in smaller numbers (50 to 200).

Potting and Seed-raising Mixes

Potting and seed-raising mixes are available in pre-mixed bags (usually about 20 litres) from nurseries and garden centres. There's a big difference in quality and certain brands are definitely superior to others. If you need only a small amount of mix, it's probably cheapest to buy a bag. If you need a little more, you can 'stretch' it by mixing it with good-quality compost and washed sand (washed sand has the fine, clogging particles removed, leaving only the coarser, free-draining ones). If you're planning to do a lot of potting, you can mix your own (see p. 29), but remember the principles of good drainage plus water-holding capacity.

Soil suppliers also deliver in bulk. If you have many tubs to fill, you can buy a bale of potting mix (why not share the cost with another gardener?) from a soil supplier, or get a trailer load from the local garden centre (though this mix is likely to be of poorer quality).

Although it's tempting, never pot plants into garden soil if you plan on keeping them in the container for any length of time—buy a quality potting mix instead. Garden soil, unless it contains a very high proportion of humus, tends to clog, set, and shrink. For precious, long-term pot plants such as azaleas and camellias, buy the best-quality mix you can find. These long-lived plants will stay in tubs for decades and you should aim to give them the best that you can.

On the other hand, it's uneconomical to buy potting mix for garden beds. Buy instead quality loams, or improve the existing soil.

Sleepers

Sleepers make attractive additions to gardens. Old railway sleepers blend beautifully with stone, soil and plants, are durable (but not as durable, of course, as stone, so bear this in mind if you're building retaining walls), but are hideously expensive and becoming more so. While travelling in central Australia I saw railway sleepers strewn like discarded toothpicks along dismantled rail lines. I thought wistfully of the trailer back home, but of course, there was a reason those sleepers were still there. The cost of hauling a ton or two of sleepers over several hundred kilometres soon puts the price of garden centre stocks into perspective.

If you're desperate for sleepers, be aware that they come in various sizes, and that although the smaller ones are cheaper you may end up paying more (because you'll need more). Calculate very carefully; work out heights, lengths, and jigsaw so you won't need to cut too many bits off ends.

Soil

Unless you're blessed with a large block or perfect soil, it's likely that at some stage of landscaping your garden you'll need to bring in extra materials. The local garden centre/landscaping supplier usually stocks a bewildering range of soils, and it can be difficult to choose which is the most appropriate. The descriptions are about as useful as the blurbs on the front of cereal packets (even less so!—the real ingredients are not listed for soils as they are on the backs of cereal packets!), so often it's impossible to know what you're getting. However, there is a key to not wasting your money: you should learn the basics of soil structure and texture. The tip on p. 60 provides an introduction, and there are numerous books that deal with the subject in greater detail (see Appendix 1).

TIP

What's in a Name: Clay, Sand or Loam?

Clay, sand and loam are simply words used to describe the texture or 'feel' of soil. Sandy soils comprise large particles that are visible to the naked eye and feel gritty. Clays have fine particles that feel silky when moistened and rubbed between the fingertips, whereas loams have medium-sized particles. Most soils comprise a mixture of particle sizes.

You can recognise soil texture by other means, too. Clay is malleable and compacts easily; when moistened and squeezed it retains its shape, whereas sand crumbles. If mixed with water, the fine particles of clay stay suspended for hours, clouding the water; the larger and heavier sand particles sink more quickly, leaving the water clear.

If you examine unimproved clay soil under the microscope, you'll see that the particles are so small that they pack tightly together, with only tiny spaces between the particles. Sandy soils, with larger grains, have much larger spaces between them.

The small spaces between the particles in compacted and unimproved clay soils are too small to allow free water movement. Water penetrates slowly and gets trapped in the spaces, causing waterlogging. In the wet season (be it winter or summer), unimproved clays become boggy, rotting the roots of most common garden plants and often killing them.

In temperate areas of Australia, summer creates a different problem. The dry heat bakes the soil in precisely the same way as clay models bake in kilns. And precisely like modelling clay, clay soils shrink, harden and crack—bad news for delicate plant roots and seedlings. In spite of this, the large surface area on all those tiny particles in clay soils holds plenty of nutrients and makes them the most productive soils on earth.

On the other hand, the large spaces between sand particles promote rapid and deep water penetration. Waterlogging is rarely a problem, but the quick flow leaches nutrients from the root zone. Unimproved sandy soils also hold, or store, little water for plants to use.

Improving Soil

Once you have a working understanding of soils, you can confidently modify them in the knowledge that you're not spending money on unnecessary or inappropriate additives. In fact, **it's almost always better to improve existing soil than to buy in new**. This is because bought soils are usually mined from deep underground and lack structure or, conversely, are taken from the surface and comprise not only excellent structure but also excellent weed seeds, which cheerfully germinate and spread through your garden.

It will take a year or two to improve existing soils (you can hurry the process by rotary hoeing in compost or additives first time), but you'll have a permanent solution—a cure, rather than a band-aid. Below is an introduction to the improvement techniques for clay and sandy soils so you won't waste money by planting into ground that can't support healthy plant growth.

Other books cover the topic of soil improvement in greater detail than I have room for here (see Appendix 1 for examples), and it's worth reading up on them. A sound understanding of the principles involved rewards you not only with a healthier bank balance but also a healthier garden.

Improving Clay Soils

Improving clay soils saves you money on water, fertiliser and plants. How? Once improved, clay soils hold plenty of water without becoming waterlogged, so you need to water less often. You'll spend less on fertiliser than in sandy soils because nutrients leach away more slowly. And you won't need to replace plants that would otherwise die through waterlogging in the wet season.

You can improve the structure of clay soils by **adding** substances to the soil. These additives make the clay friable (crumbly), preventing compaction and creating those spaces so essential for water movement. However, never dig or work clay soils when they're very wet because this worsens compaction and wrecks structure.

Gypsum is outstanding in improving most clay soils. Sprinkled over cloddy clay soils at the rate of about 500 grams per square metre, gypsum gradually makes the tiny individual clay particles clump together. It's cheap, easy to apply and—contrary to popular belief—doesn't significantly change the pH of the soil.

Humus (organic matter) also makes heavy clays friable, encouraging aggregate formation in the same way as does gypsum. The bits of organic matter act as tiny sponges, holding water and separating the clay aggregates. Because the aim is to improve soil structure, rather than to add nutrients, bulky humus, in the form of compost or green manures, is preferable to lower volume, more quickly broken down animal manures (see Chapter 7 for more information on manures).

Sand, in the form of coarse river sand, is good for small areas but must be mixed very thoroughly (rotary hoed) to prevent pockets of poor drainage. Beware also fine, silty sands sold by many garden centres. A combination of compost and gypsum is usually more effective.

Liquid clay breakers and soil wetters are especially effective in established areas or on lawns where you don't want to dig or hoe, but these innocuous-sounding chemicals can be deadly to frogs. Never use them near ponds or watercourses. Dilute at the recommended rate and apply with a watering can, avoiding run-off.

Improving Sandy Soils
As for clay soils, improving sandy soils saves you money on fertilisers and plants, but especially on water.

Humus (in the form of bulky composts) is still the best way to improve sandy soils. Add humus, then add more, and then add still more (see pp. 48, 57 for cheap sources of humus).

Mulching reduces evaporation on porous sandy soils, and adds valuable humus as it breaks down (see pp. 48, 57 for cheap mulches).

Clay may be added (this was traditionally known as 'marling'), but must be mixed very thoroughly if it's to have a beneficial effect and not merely sit around as hard lumps in the sand. Water-repellent sands are best treated by marling.

Buying Soil
Sometimes you'll have to bite the bullet and *buy* soil. You may be on a building site where all the topsoil has been removed, and you lack the time or opportunity of getting free 'clean fill' (see p. 62). You may wish to establish a rose, vegetable or special-purpose garden where you need to be sure that the soil you're getting is appropriate. This applies especially if you're establishing a lawn, when skimping is definitely false economy. Growing lawn on fill, bedrock or heavy clay is inevitably disastrous. Get advice from the lawn specialists in your town and follow it to the letter. Scrooging on either quality or quantity of soil for lawn will see years of hassles with drainage, compaction, fungal problems, impenetrability, poor fertility and growth, so that although establishing your lawn might have been cheaper, you'll spend ten times that amount in maintaining it for years down the track.

Sandy loams are generally seen as ideal soils for most home garden conditions because they suit a wide range of plants, hold nutrients well and drain readily. Unfortunately, many soils sold as 'sandy loams' are, in fact, sandy clays and contain little or no humus (see p. 60). This is a problem, because after wetting, the fine clay particles bond together, giving your garden bed the appearance and texture of a concrete slab. The soil surface is impermeable and horrible to work—hard and cloddy instead of soft and crumbly. Consult an independent knowledgeable person (*not* the landscape supplier), or pay extra to get a blend with a generous mix of humus.

Fill

You might have seen signs dotted about suburbia where hopeful gardeners request 'clean fill'. Anyone wanting to get rid of a load of rubble or excavated soil dumps it, free, on the hopeful gardener's doorstep. The idea is a good one, but all too often the fill is not clean at all but contaminated with building rubble, wire, glass, weeds and old boots. Dirty fill is acceptable for 'filling', but unacceptable for most garden beds, especially if you're going to be poking about in it with your bare hands. Of course it's free but you take your chances. You can't complain if you get what you haven't paid for.

Sub-bases

Gravel, dolomite and builders' sand are expensive, but unfortunately there are few alternatives. These materials are generally chosen to provide a firm, compacted base or to improve drainage around structures. Choosing inferior alternatives is likely to prove false economy when your carport floods or your tennis court begins to resemble a choppy sea instead of a bowling green.

Stone and Rock

When establishing our own garden, my partner and I took the trailer to a local quarry and selected our own rocks at a fraction of the cost of buying them from a retail outlet. We bought crazy-pave slate from a supplier that specialised in providing masonry for headstones; the slate offcuts we bought were broken and therefore unsuitable for most of his regular buyers ... but perfect for us.

If you have friends with acreages, you may be able to collect weathered rocks from their land, but be aware of the environmental damage you may be doing. Rocks provide homes for wildlife and indiscriminate removal reduces the biological diversity of a local area. A few rocks here or there won't make a significant difference, but denuding an area will. One of my pet hates is the large-scale removal of 'moss rocks' from properties. Not only does this destroy what little is left of the original ecology of the area, but the moss on the rocks is in fact lichen; when the rocks are repositioned in a shady, 'mossy' site in someone's garden, the lichen (adapted to very specific climatic conditions) promptly dies. Environmentally aware gardeners don't buy moss rocks from a garden centre; in fact, they don't use them at all.

TIP

Changing soil pH

Soil pH is a measure of its acidity (like vinegar) or alkalinity (like bicarbonate of soda). pH is measured on a scale of 0 (extremely acid) to 14 (extremely alkaline) with 7 being neutral. Most soils fall in the range of pH 4.5 to 8 and certain plants have preferences for certain pH ranges. You can change soil pH by one point by adding lime (to increase pH), peat or various sulphur compounds (to decrease pH). However, it's uneconomical to change pH by much more than one point, because the pH scale is logarithmic, with each point being ten times higher than the one before. Instead, choose plants that like the pH of your existing soil, or use pots.

Pest Control

Chemical or Organic?

Nothing gets gardeners hotter under the collar than arguments about correct fertiliser and pesticide use. There are the old-guard sledgehammer proponents (*hit 'em with the napalm, and why not double the concentration, just to be sure?*) and the born-again and new-age proponents (*the bugs have a right to be there too*). Indeed they do, *but...*

Many proponents of organic gardening suggest that organic pesticides and fertilisers are 'softer' on the environment than chemical ones. This is often, but by no means always, the case. Many organic pesticides, such as derris dust, aren't target-specific, and are deadly to bees, fish or worms. Often, organic fertilisers contain the same active ingredients as chemical ones, but are far more expensive per volume/weight. Of course, this means that it's easy to overfertilise plants with chemical fertilisers ... but chicken and other 'hot' organic manures are notorious for their ability to burn plants, too. Sometimes, organic pesticides require an intensity of labour that you just can't afford (daily applications can become tedious).

My own approach is a combination of organic and chemical methods. Wherever possible, I'll use the organic solution, backed

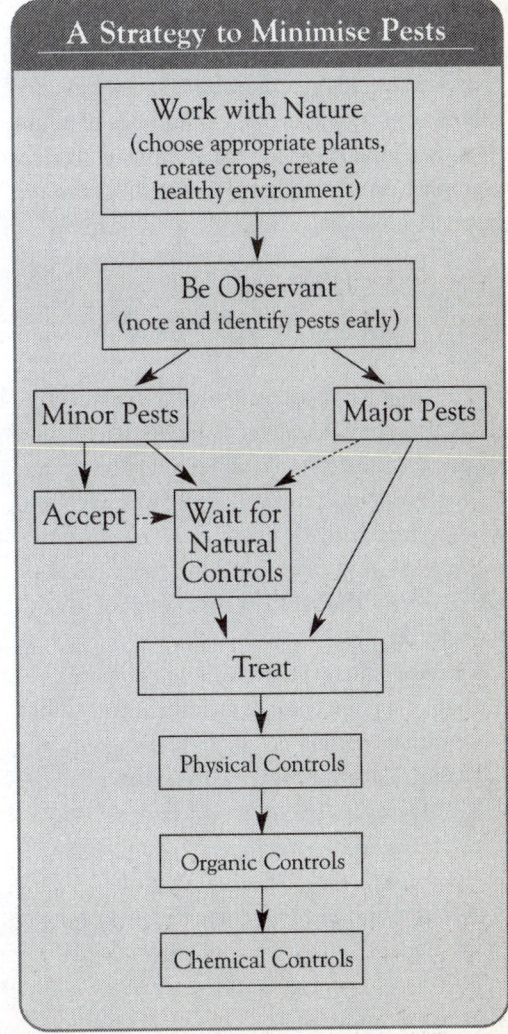

A Strategy to Minimise Pests

Work with Nature
(choose appropriate plants, rotate crops, create a healthy environment)
↓
Be Observant
(note and identify pests early)
↓
Minor Pests → Major Pests

Accept → Wait for Natural Controls

Treat

Physical Controls

Organic Controls

Chemical Controls

by a chemical one if necessary. For example, I dust tomato plants with a combination of sulphur (organic fungicide) and derris (organic insecticide), but control millipedes with snail pellets. And sometimes you can use chemicals when quick results are important, followed by organic methods. Be flexible in your approach.

Remember, too, that pest control needn't be wholesale slaughter with the equivalent of aerial drenching by a crop-duster. Picking off caterpillars and snails as you see them is often sufficient in small gardens, or when you grow only a few tomato plants. And I urge every gardener to read the classic *Silent Spring* by Rachel Carson before they buy their first bottle of pesticide.

Everyone has their own stance on pesticide use, and it's an area where you'll have to follow your own star. Still, principles of commonsense and compromise apply here as they do elsewhere in life. Steer your own course, but below are suggestions gleaned from my own experience.

Working with Nature

It's always easier swimming with the current than against it: wherever possible, you should work *with* nature. You don't need to adopt a full-on permaculture approach (where your whole garden ideally becomes a self-sustaining ecosystem), but it certainly helps to take advantage of the sensible principles of permaculture.

1. **Choose plants, cultivars and rootstocks that suit your climate and soil.** They'll be healthier and more disease-resistant than plants that are struggling to adapt to a hostile environment (you'd choose cacti, not ferns, for a garden in arid central Australia).
2. **Avoid monocultures** (many plants of the same species planted close together—a free buffet for pests and diseases).
3. **Scrupulously rotate crops** in vegetable gardens to minimise the build-up of soil-borne diseases.
4. **Observe basic hygiene.** Trim off and dispose of diseased plant material (especially fungal diseases) promptly. When pruning roses and fruiting plants, dip secateurs in methylated spirits between bushes.
5. **Be observant.** Many diseases and pests are easy to control if you treat them in their early stages, before they've spread throughout the garden. On the other hand, accept, if you can, a few insect pests. A garden devoid of a single insect pest is as unnatural as a sterile one. As for birds and caterpillars, only you know what percentage of your harvest you're prepared to share (but seriously, do a few holes in the lettuce leaves really matter?).
6. **Accept, if you can, a few weeds (but try to remove them before they seed).** I've seen pristine gardens devoid of any visible weeds but, once again, it's a matter of personal taste whether you prefer this effect. It's only when weeds compete with or crowd out the plants you want to grow that they become a problem. It depends also on how much time you have available to weed, although bear in mind that a regularly maintained, well-mulched garden sports fewer weeds over the years than a neglected one. I've seen even stubborn weeds like oxalis and, incredibly, sorrel all but eliminated from a garden through judicious hand-weeding.

Physical Insect Control

Physical controls are relatively high in labour but low in cost. Rather than using chemicals, you control pests by physically squashing, trapping, barring or removing them. These techniques are especially effective against snails, slugs, and large caterpillars. Squash them whenever you see them (going out with a torch at night is helpful), or construct traps. A wooden board laid flat and sup-

ported at each end with stones to maintain a
1.5–2-centimetre clearance provides an
attractive shelter for snails and slugs. Lift the
plank and squash pests regularly. Place bait
(cut potato, bran, lettuce, hollowed-out
citrus) under an upturned pot in a shady spot.
Clear regularly. Use pest-repelling mulches
or barriers (flour, oak leaves and copper
strips) around stems of plants.

You can remove those pesky, sap-sucking
aphids quickly and effectively from robust
tub plants or shrubs by using a high-pressure
squirt of water from the hose. This needs to
be done every three days or so in warm
weather, but take care: it's possible to snap
tender growing shoots of certain plants.

Encouraging natural predators (e.g. wasps,
spiders, mantises and ladybirds), netting trees
and currants against birds, and setting traps
(for fruit fly) are just a few practical and
cheap physical controls available not only to
dedicated organic gardeners but those who
want a healthy garden.

Some gardeners swear by companion
plants. Although this technique can
undoubtedly improve pollination (by attracting bees), soil fertility (by complementary
nutrient uptake or release), provide shelter
for 'good' insects and reduce soil-borne pests
by the release of certain chemicals, I have yet
to see first-hand its efficacy in *repelling* pests
above-ground. I'll concede that a handker-
chief-sized vegetable garden in the middle of
two hectares of pyrethrum might, indeed,
suffer fewer insect pests. However, the worst

black aphid infestation to ever occur in my
garden was on chives planted amongst my
vegetables to deter … yes, you've guessed it.
Did the chives act as a sacrifice trap, attracting the aphids away from the vegetables?
Maybe. It was difficult to tell; there were too
many aphids on everything else.

On the other hand, marigolds (*Tagetes*
species, not *Calendula* species) are reliably
reported to inhibit root-knot and eelworms
in the soil—grown together with, or before,
vegetable crops they reduce the populations
of these soil-borne pests. And asparagus
releases chemicals that inhibit nematodes on
tomatoes. If you have the space, companion
planting is worth a try.

Physical Weed Control

Physical weed control generally means
elbow grease—yours. You physically remove
the weeds, rather than spraying them with
chemicals.

The trick for successful physical weed
control is *regular maintenance*. Easy enough to
say, I know. But regular and judicious hand-
weeding removes plants before they have a
chance to form seed. Of course, there's a
huge reservoir of seeds in topsoil, and they
blow in from everywhere, but annual weeds,
and many perennial weeds, can usually be
controlled in a normal-sized home garden by
hand-weeding.

Most keen gardeners I know admit to
finding a quiet hour or two of weeding quite
relaxing and therapeutic. But not everyone
has the luxury of time to hand-weed, and
persistent perennial weeds (especially those
with underground runners, bulbs or tubers
such as soursob, sorrel and couch grass) can
be discouraging as they'll regrow from the
tiniest remnant. Still, I've seen perennial
weeds controlled (not eliminated) from a
smallish suburban garden after judicious
weeding, but most of us are not quite so
fanatical. In the case of persistent perennial

Living Mulches

(vigorous enough to smother most weeds)

Achillea spp. (yarrows)*
Ajuga 'Jungle Beauty'
Aptenia cordifolia
Arctotis × *hybrida* (Aurora Daisy)
Campanula posharskyana
Cerastium tomentosum (Snow in Summer)
Convolvulus mauriticanus
Coprosma kirkii
Duchesnia indica (Mock Strawberry)*
Grevillea × *gaudichaudii*
Hebe veronica
Hypericum calycinum
Juniperinus procumbens, J. conferta
Lamium maculatum (Creeping Dead Nettle)
Lamiastrum galeobdolen (Aluminium Plant)
Lantana montevidensis
Lysimachia nummularia (Moneywort)*
Myoporum parvifolium
Osteospermum fruticosum
Ophiopogon japonicus (Mondo Grass)*
Polygonum capitatum
Prunella vulgaris (Self Heal)*
Rosmarinus officinalis 'Prostratus' (Prostrate Rosemary)
Saponaria ocymoides (Rock Soapwort)
Saxifraga stolonifera
Stachys byzantina (Lamb's Ears)
Vinca majus (Larger Periwinkle)*
V. minor (Lesser Periwinkle)*
Viola odorata (Sweet Violet)*

* Denotes very vigorous groundcovers, though this varies with geographic location and microclimate. These groundcovers smother weeds, but may also smother other plants or become weeds themselves! Use with care.

weeds, you'll probably want to use a chemical herbicide.

Weeds near vegetable gardens can shelter pests like slugs and snails, so it's best to control weeds near sensitive areas.

If you're establishing a new area, you can thickly sprinkle a 'hot' fertiliser (urea or sulphate of ammonia) or manure (pigeon or chicken) on the weeds and, if you can, cover them with black or clear plastic on a hot, sunny day. Leave in place for a week. This has the effect of cooking the exposed growth, but be aware that the concentrated salts can also damage the soil microflora and fauna. And deep-rooted perennial weeds may survive this treatment. Still, it's worth doing if your weeds aren't persistent ones and if you can establish new plants quickly to provide competition and to prevent the original weeds reestablishing.

Mulching is a highly effective weed-control technique (see pp. 48–9 for cheap mulches). So is planting with groundcover species vigorous enough to smother weeds (see left). If you like the cottage garden effect, let self-seeding flowering plants spread

Naturalising Annuals and Perennials to Replace Weeds

Check your local area to see what will thrive in your climate.

Aquilegia spp. (columbines)
Centaurea cyanus (Cornflower)
Digitalis purpurea (Foxglove)
Iberis amara (Candytuft)
Lunaria annua (Honesty)
Myosotis and *Cynoglossum* spp. (forget-me-nots)
Nigella damascena (Love-in-the-Mist)
Oenothera biennis (Evening Primrose)
Rhodanthe anthemoides (Paper Daisy)
Tropaeolum major (Nasturtium)
Viola tricolor (Heartsease)

between shrubs and across bare ground. It takes a few years of selective weeding, but you'll gradually increase the proportion of flowers to weeds. See the box on p. 66 for naturalising annuals and perennials. Be aware, though, that some of the more vigorous flowers may become weeds themselves!

Weeding Tools

I find a plasterer's knife indispensable for weeding. It is lighter, more versatile and cheaper than a traditional forked weed-lifter. As it wears, the blade becomes smaller, easier to use and sharper, actually increasing its efficiency! What more can you ask of a tool? You can also try using an ordinary kitchen knife or a trowel.

Hoeing is a cheap and effective technique but seems to be a lost art in these days of herbicide sprays. The trick is to slide the hoe just under the soil surface in a shallow chopping motion, lifting the weeds so the roots are exposed without digging deeply into the subsoil. Choose a dry, warm day so the roots dry quickly, or hoe often enough to prevent the weeds regrowing.

Chemical Pesticides

If the grubs are taking over your garden and you despair of having any fruit or flowers left, it may be time to consider some form of pest control other than squashing individual insects. Pesticides are substances that kill

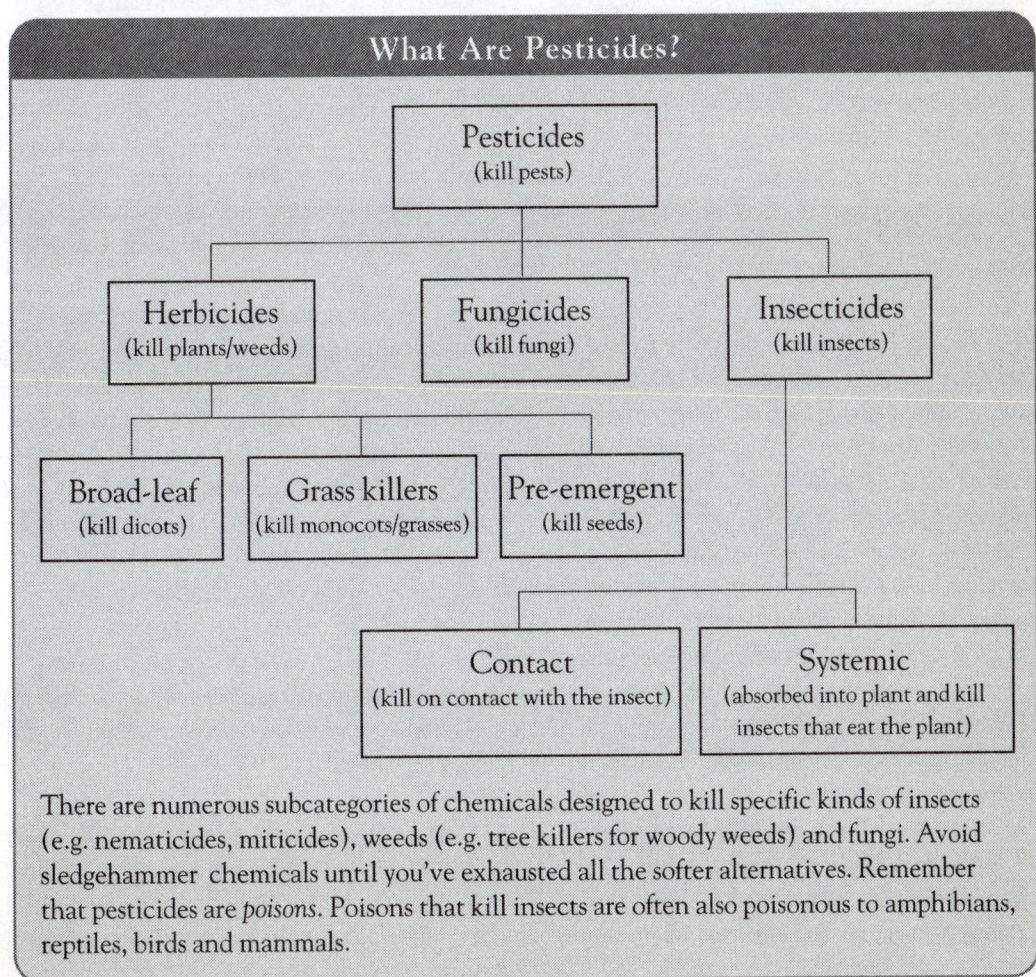

What Are Pesticides?

There are numerous subcategories of chemicals designed to kill specific kinds of insects (e.g. nematicides, miticides), weeds (e.g. tree killers for woody weeds) and fungi. Avoid sledgehammer chemicals until you've exhausted all the softer alternatives. Remember that pesticides are *poisons*. Poisons that kill insects are often also poisonous to amphibians, reptiles, birds and mammals.

pests. They include **insecticides** (for insects), **fungicides** (for fungi or moulds), and **herbicides** (for weeds). Certain specific pesticides target bacterial diseases, mites and nematodes, but these are more likely to be used by commercial growers.

Pesticides range from the highly toxic and persistent (indeed, Australia has a depressing history of continuing to use nasty pesticides like organochlorines long after they've been banned in other parts of the world) to very mild and short-term (garlic sprays, soapy water).

Systemic insecticides are absorbed by the leaves and circulate through the plant. They have the advantage of killing only those bugs that munch on the plant. **Contact insecticides** kill any insects they touch (or sometimes only soft-bodied insects like caterpillars)—not good if you're trying to build up a population of natural insect predators (such as ladybirds, wasps, spiders and mantises).

The Importance of Targeting

When using pesticides, it's essential to first accurately identify your pest. This sounds obvious, but I know gardeners (no names mentioned!) who have bought expensive chemical insecticides only to discover three weeks later that their plants were infected with a *fungal* disease! So before buying or implementing any cure—conventional or organic—be sure you've diagnosed the disease; this is known as 'targeting'. Most nursery staff will happily identify plant pests (but remember to bring your specimen in a *sealed* plastic bag if you don't want to be chased off the premises), as will some Botanic Gardens' Home Gardens Advisory Services (see Appendix 3) or the appropriate Government department (see Appendix 4).

The importance of targeting applies equally to herbicides. Some are specific to certain plant groups and you need to be sure you've purchased the correct one: '**broad-leaf' herbicides** kill certain weeds in lawns, grass killers kill grasses in garden beds, and '**pre-emergent' herbicides** kill seeds. Although herbicides are generally less toxic to mammals, fish, birds and reptiles than are insecticides, you should always exercise extreme care when spraying, not only for your own health but that of the environment in general. Even herbicides that are considered non-persistent and of low toxicity have subsequently been shown to have severe effects on fish, frogs, or birds (see again Rachel Carson's *Silent Spring* for a chilling chronicle of non-target effects). Glyphosate is a relatively new herbicide considered very safe (and indeed it breaks down very quickly on contact with the soil), but unfortunately the wetting agent it was originally mixed with killed frogs even when present in very low concentrations. In fact, most wetting agents are deadly to frogs, so don't spray around your pond (suburbia is an important habitat for frogs), or if you live near watercourses.

Beware the term 'environmentally friendly'. Friendly compared to *what*? Napalm? A pesticide is by definition designed to kill living things. While researching this book, I came across a new pesticide with a name designed to inspire confidence in the buyer, and labelled 'environmentally friendly'. 'Won't harm non-target species and beneficial insects', the display stand blared, below which, in much smaller letters, was written, 'when used as directed'. The back of the pesticide pack advised, 'DO NOT allow chemical containers or spray to get into drains, sewers, streams or ponds. DO NOT spray if bees are feeding on flowering plants. Will kill bees'. Indeed.

Always follow safety directions when using pesticides.

Kill the Pests, Not Your Kids: Safe Pesticide Use

These directions apply to the more toxic organic pesticides as well as the chemical ones. Swallowing copper oxychloride will make you as sick, if not more sick, than many of the non-organic pesticides.

1. Read safety directions carefully.
2. Follow them.
3. Don't spray in windy weather.
4. Wear protective clothing—try not to let pesticides touch your skin and avoid breathing in the dust or spray mist.
5. Keep pesticides in their original containers.
6. Don't use pesticides past their use-by date no matter how much you want to save money.
7. No matter how much you'd like to save money, don't buy second-hand or poor-quality spray equipment.
8. Dispose of old pesticides (take them to a depot; don't pour down drains).
9. Wash yourself and your equipment thoroughly after spraying.
10. Use separate spray equipment for herbicides and insecticides.
11. Don't eat, drink or smoke while applying pesticides.
12. Store pesticides in a cool, dry place out of reach of children and animals.

Value for Money

As with aspirin, sneakers, and underwear whose waistbands prominently feature the designer's moniker, you can get sucked into paying for the brand name rather than the product in the pesticide market. Gram for gram, home-brand glyphosate is as effective as brand-name glyphosate (like home-brand aspirin compared with Aspro™). As you would in the supermarket, you need to assess value for money by determining the amount of active ingredient you're actually getting

TIP

Calculating Value for Money
Compare two bottles of pyrethrin insecticide:

Bottle A: Sledgehammer Bug Zapper
   Total volume: 500 mL
   Active ingredient: 4 g per L pyrethrins
   Price: $10
   Total amount of active ingredient in 500 mL bottle is 2 g
   Price = $5 per g

Bottle B: Mass Slaughter Insect Spray
   Total volume: 250 mL
   Active ingredient: 16 g per L pyrethrins
   Price: $15
   Total amount of active ingredient in 250 mL bottle is 4 g
   Price = $3.75 per g.

Bottle B represents better value for money.

I visited my local garden centre and, using the above technique, compared prices of competing products that had the same active ingredient.
White oil (an insecticide that kills scale insects) products ranged in price from 3c per gram to 8c per gram.
Maldison (an insecticide) products ranged from 9c per gram to 47c per gram.
Glyphosate (a herbicide) products ranged from 8c per gram to $2.70 per gram.
Dimethoate (an insecticide) ranged from 30c per gram to $82.86 per gram.
Pyrethrin (an insecticide) products ranged from 80c per gram to an eye-popping $125.83 per gram!
In many cases, even huge price differences are not obvious until the sums are done. Usually (but not always), ready-to-use products that have been premixed with water are more expensive than those you mix yourself.

See Appendix 6 for more information on pesticides.

for your dollar. This can be a little tricky, and if your algebra's not too flash you'd be well advised to take along a pencil and paper or calculator when you shop.

Read and compare the labels of competing products carefully. What you're paying for is the *active ingredient* (the chemical that's doing the killing). Don't be misled by the size of the container—a large one may have a lower concentration of active ingredient, so you need to use a larger volume when you mix the product at home. Some labels cite the amount of active ingredient in grams per litre, or milligrams per 100 millilitres, or millilitres per 500 millilitres. When the volumes in the containers themselves also differ, it can get confusing (see Tip on p. 69).

Bulk buying can save you even more money, but beware. Large containers aimed at the agricultural market generally provide the best active-ingredient-per-dollar rate, and buying a ten year supply might sound like good economic sense. Unfortunately, most pesticides have a use-by date, and in two years you might have to throw out eight-tenths of the bottle. Pesticides should never be poured down the drain. Instead, you have to pay to take them to a special toxic waste depot in your area. There goes your bargain.

Never try to save money by spraying pesticide past its use-by date or, worse, by using a pesticide whose label has so faded and discoloured that you can no longer read the name or other details. Even if you think you can remember the contents and the instructions, don't take the risk. Near enough is *not* good enough—for you or the environment.

Never vary the recommended dilution rate for any chemical pesticides. By doing so you may kill non-target species (bees, worms, and small children). If overdiluting, you may promote pest resistance to the pesticide by leaving a portion of the population alive to breed.

Home Remedies

You can make many cheap pesticides yourself at home. Chilli, coriander, eucalyptus oil, flour, garlic, mustard seeds, onion, wormwood and many other substances in combination with or without soap or other wetting agents can be made into sprays to kill and/or deter pests. Generally, their toxicity is low and they have low persistence, so need to be reapplied frequently. Books specialising in natural pest control list recipes (see Appendix 1 for good books on pest control).

CHAPTER 7

Fertilisers

Why Fertilise?

For plants to thrive and to look lush and healthy, you'll need to improve and maintain the nutrient balance in your garden.

Like people, plants require food, water and vitamins to grow. To extend the analogy, consider the 'food' of plants to be sunlight, water and carbon dioxide, while their vitamins are absorbed from the soil (via their roots) or through their leaves (when you apply soluble fertilisers). Just as people can live on a diet of honey sandwiches for some time (if you don't believe this to be the case, just ask the parent of any toddler), most garden plants can survive with only sunlight, carbon dioxide and water for many months, without any *added* nutrients. Unfortunately, a diet comprising only honey sandwiches is not conducive to human health. Without a proper balance of vitamins skin grows sallow, digestion clogs and internal organs misfunction. Eventually, a diet of honey sandwiches poisons people as effectively as does arsenic.

Plants are no different. Without an adequate and balanced nutrient supply, your plants actually look 'sick', with pale leaves, few flowers and poor fruit. Plants also succumb to disease attack more readily, and die prematurely. A basic understanding of

the principles of plant nutrition is, I believe, absolutely essential if you don't want to waste money on plants whose only destiny is to languish and die. Similarly, understanding the principles of plant nutrition will help you supply the fertiliser (i.e. vitamin supplement) that's needed, and you won't waste money on overfertilising or applying the incorrect nutrient. The box on p. 72 lists the major plant nutrients, their role in plant growth, and describes deficiency symptoms.

Like pesticides, fertilisers fall into two broad categories: **chemical** and **organic**. The latter is promoted by purists as being softer on the environment, but this is not always the case and the differences can be academic. The nitrogen in inappropriately applied fresh chook manure will burn plants and worms as easily as the nitrogen in chemically manufactured sulphate of ammonia.

Fertilisers may be further subdivided into **balanced** or **specific** categories. Balanced fertilisers are equivalent to a multivitamin pill. They contain a balance of the major nutrients required by plants, plus the trace elements (trace elements are nutrients required by plants in tiny quantities—see box on p. 72). A classic example of a balanced *chemical* fertiliser is 'Complete D'; a balanced *organic* fertiliser is good-quality cow manure.

71

Plant Nutrients

The Primary Nutrients

Nitrogen (N)

Nitrogen is essential for healthy plant growth, particularly of leaves and stems. It is needed throughout the entire season but especially during major growth periods (spring). Deficiency symptoms occur first in the oldest leaves and include yellowing, stunting, and premature death. Deficiency occurs most commonly in soils that are sandy, leached, very wet or have never been improved with compost or nitrogenous fertilisers.

Too much nitrogen results in excessively soft, lush growth that's prone to insect attack and wilting in warm weather. If you give fruit, flowers and vegetables too much nitrogen, you'll end up with lush leaves but few or no flowers and fruit.

Phosphorus (P)

Phosphorus is an essential component in most plant biochemical interactions and the healthy development of roots. Almost all Australian soils are low in phosphorus (with the exception of those that have been improved with phosphoric fertilisers). Deficiency symptoms include stunted, erect growth, with the older leaves yellowing and often tinged with blue-green or purple colours. Native plants, unsurprisingly, are less susceptible to phosphorus deficiencies (indeed, many find phosphorus toxic), but you'll need to supplement for exotic ornamentals and vegetables.

Potassium (K)

Potassium plays an important role in the production of flowers and fruit and in protecting plants from disease—it's the equivalent of our immune system. Deficiency is most common in sandy soils, in high rainfall areas, or areas that have been cropped for a long time without replenishment of nutrients. Deficiency symptoms occur on the oldest leaves first and include scorched, brown margins and spots surrounded by pale haloes. Vegetables and fruiting trees generally need relatively high levels of potassium.

N:P:K Ratio

The N:P:K ratio is the proportions of the three major nutrients and is usually listed as percentages on fertiliser packages.

Secondary Nutrients and Trace Elements

Calcium, magnesium and sulphur are needed in smaller quantities for healthy plant growth. The trace elements—iron, manganese, copper, molybdenum, boron, zinc and cobalt—are required in still tinier amounts. Regular composting and mulching with good materials is likely to produce sufficient secondary and trace elements in all but the most deficient and unbalanced of soils.

Specific fertilisers are the equivalent of, say, a vitamin C capsule. Specific chemical fertilisers include urea, sulphate of ammonia and sulphate of potash.

Balanced fertilisers are generally safe to use because it's difficult to overdose plants (as in humans, an excess of one nutrient can impede the absorption or processing of another, leading to complex deficiency symptoms). On the other hand, specific deficiencies in particular plants (e.g. those which have exceptionally high potash requirements to produce fruit) or soil types (Australian soils are notoriously low in phosphorus) can be quickly and effectively cured by the application of a specific fertiliser. Remember, though, that the healthiest plant growth will generally occur in healthy soil that has been built up with copious amounts of organic matter (see pp. 48, 57). Such soil has a naturally high nutrient balance and flourishing microflora and fauna that aid in the breakdown of nutrients so that they are made available to plant roots. Applying highly concentrated or specific fertilisers to soil can, in some circumstances, severely damage the microflora. Remember that twice the recommended dose won't give twice the result. Instead, you're likely to cause all sorts of problems, the simplest of which is burning. Too much nitrogen can cause potassium deficiency, too much phosphorus can cause potassium and zinc deficiencies, and so on.

As when selecting pesticides, you should identify the problem (in this case, nutrient deficiency), before selecting your fertiliser (see p 72).

You can then choose the fertiliser that most effectively treats the deficiency.

I believe a balanced approach is best for fertilisers as it is for pesticides. I feed my currant bushes with a heavy mulch of chicken manure and compost, but boost this with a sprinkling of sulphate of potash to balance the high-nitrogen content of the mulch. I top-dress and mulch tub plants with chicken compost too, but supplement with foliar fertiliser and slow-release balanced fertiliser as necessary. Purists will need to do their research to give their plants a balanced diet.

Organic Fertilisers

The advantage of organic fertilisers is that it's often possible to find cheap, high-quality sources that cost nothing more than a bit of elbow grease. Organic fertilisers promote healthy soil microflora, and many have little-understood but well-documented synergistic effects, where the improvement in plant growth is more than can be explained by the actual nutrient content of the fertiliser.

Because organic fertilisers are natural products and not manufactured in laboratories, they are not 'pure' products but contain a mixture of nutrients, trace elements and impurities. Specific organic fertilisers are therefore rare.

Animal Manures

Animal manures are excellent fertilisers, and the bulkier ones also improve soil structure. If you're lucky enough to have family or friends who let you collect manure from their properties, be courteous. If you're offering to clean out the pen or coop, clean *all* of it. Don't take half because that's all you want, or you're sick of shovelling.

Be guided by your friend's needs, as well as your own. You could, for example, offer to spread half of what you gather on their garden for them, especially if the friend is elderly or infirm. Alternatively, offer some payment; the amount will depend on your own and your friend's circumstances. Check the going rate in garden centres, and offer, say, half that. Payment in kind is another option: fresh produce from your garden (jam, sauce, fruit or vegetables, or seeds) is welcomed by most friends. Still, if you want your friends to remain so, don't be cheap or greedy. Match their generosity with your own.

Primary producers (dairy, sheep and chook farmers) work damn hard for a living, and I think it's exceptionally rude to exploit them by expecting free produce, even though you're collecting it yourself and may be doing them a favour by cleaning their pens. Always offer some fair payment (monetary or in kind), unless you want to lie awake nights.

Chicken Manure
With the exception of pigeon manure, chook manure has a higher nitrogen concentration than any other commonly available manure.

It also contains phosphorus and potassium in smaller amounts.

Chooks may be regarded as a free fertiliser factory in your backyard, and anyone serious about saving money should have half a dozen hens scratching about. Once you've built the coop, there's little extra cost, though you may want to supplement the hens' diet with laying pellets.

Keeping chooks will save you money in all kinds of ways. You'll get free eggs, and dispose of kitchen scraps with less mess and flies than when you throw them on a compost heap.

Throw green weeds and fine prunings into the coop as well—in six months they'll have rotted down to a rich fertiliser that can be applied directly to garden beds (see pp. 76–9 for more information on composting and mulching).

If you want to save money on fertiliser in your garden, chooks probably represent the best investment you can make (see also p. 103 on planning for chook sheds).

You may be able to get free manure from friends by offering to clean their coops out for them, but don't hold your breath. Poultry manure is justifiably famous among gardeners, and anyone who keeps chooks is likely to fully appreciate the value of their asset.

Cow Manure

A bulkier manure with about one-third the nitrogen percentage of poultry manure, moo poo is outstanding for improving soil structure. It's also relatively 'balanced', with about 1 per cent nitrogen, 0.4 per cent phosphorus and 0.5 per cent potassium. It's available bagged, sterilised and sieved from garden centres but the price is astronomical when you consider the amounts you need. It's uneconomical to buy moo poo this way—better to buy an inorganic balanced fertiliser and bulk up with garden compost.

If you're lucky enough to know a dairy farmer, offer to clean out the area outside the milking shed, which usually boasts a heavy build-up of manure—much more than the farmer is likely to use herself. You'll probably get quite a few trailer loads (moos produce *lots* of poo) so organise a place to compost it at home well beforehand. Wear rubber boots.

You may also be able to gather cow pats from the paddock. This is tedious, but not as tedious as it sounds. Either way, if you're prepared to put in the elbow grease, gathering moo poo represents excellent value for money. Moo poo is best composted hot for a month or two before spreading in the garden to help destroy weed seeds (see Composting in this chapter).

Horse Manure

My grandfather regularly took me to the local horse stables to collect the manure. It cost about $5 per trailer load, and we had to shovel it from a deep brick pen. The ammonia was so strong it made my eyes water. Horse manure contains slightly less nitrogen than cow manure but has the same concentrations of phosphorus and potassium, and makes excellent fertiliser. It's worth visiting your local stables, or offering to clean up for horse-owning friends. Horses don't have as many stomachs as cows and their manure contains more viable seeds. You should always compost horse manure for three to six months before use; pile it into a bay so that it generates plenty of heat to kill as many seeds as possible (see Composting in this chapter).

Pigeon Manure

Pigeon manure is an excellent fertiliser but very strong, with about 5 per cent nitrogen and five to six times the concentration of phosphorus and potassium as cow and horse manure. Your best bet would be to contact the local pigeon fancier's club. This fertiliser is so rich that if you have a chance to get some you shouldn't quibble about paying for it. Be prepared with a price if asked (but first check with a few garden centres so you know the going rates) and be grateful.

Sheep Manure

Sheep manure is another excellent fertiliser. It has the same concentration of phosphorus and potassium as horse and cow manure, but falls somewhere between the two in its nitrogen content. You may be able to collect sheep manure from shearing pens after shearing time, but the best stuff comes from under the sheds where there may be a build-up from decades, and tens of thousands, of sheep. Many smart farmers have cottoned on to selling this wonderful compost to suppliers but, if you know a hobby farmer, you might be able to get some sheep manure at a modest price if you're prepared to get in and muck out yourself.

Other Manures

Unusual manures are usually not worth paying for, but great if you can get them free. Zoo poo is a great marketing gimmick (you're fertilising your vegies with elephant poo) but is, for obvious reasons, variable in quality.

Guinea pigs and rabbits produce vast quantities of poo for such small creatures; it's slow to break down but, if you have access to it, is worth using.

Pig manure is low in potassium but otherwise excellent, though it should be composted thoroughly as it harbours some diseases.

Dog manure is high in nutrients, too. For obvious reasons, you should compost it thoroughly in an anaerobic system or Gedye bin before use (see Composting in this chapter). Or just dig holes around the garden, bury it in place, and let the worms and soil microflora do the work.

Human waste is used as a fertiliser in many countries, but health regulations prohibit its use in Australia. The exception is composting toilets, which reduce human waste to a rich, excellent fertiliser. If you have the luck to have access to it, put away your squeamishness and use it. You'll just be returning to the soil what you take away in crops.

Bat guano is terrific (10 per cent nitrogen, 4 per cent available phosphorus), as is dried blood (13 per cent nitrogen, 2 per cent phosphorus, 1 per cent potassium), but these fertilisers are usually available only to Transylvanian counts.

Blood and Bone

Blood and bone is high in nitrogen and phosphorus, but doesn't contain potassium. It is generally an excellent fertiliser for normal garden use, but expensive.

Composts

Composts generally comprise well-rotted/broken down organic materials. They can be used as mulch, but are more often mixed into the soil. They promote healthy plants by:

1. improving drainage in heavy soils
2. improving aeration
3. improving the water-holding capacity of sandy soils
4. improving water penetration
5. promoting a healthy soil microflora and fauna
6. supplying plant nutrients

Many mulch materials can be composted first and then dug into the garden. Sawdust is too woody to be dug in fresh, but if composted for a month or two with a generous amount of chicken manure it makes wonderful, crumbly compost.

You can buy plenty of expensive mulches and composts from garden centres: pine chips in a huge range of sizes, pine bark, hardwood chips, spent mushroom compost and other specialised composts. These are generally of excellent quality but by their very nature bulky—you'll need large amounts to get any benefit. One of the ironies of gardening is that often it's when you need compost most that you have the least: in new gardens with little or no established plant growth you'll

> **Composting** is simply the speeding up of the natural rotting process that all organic material undergoes.

need to import compost and mulch, whereas a well-established garden generates large amounts of both compost and mulch in the form of leaves, prunings, weeds and lawn clippings.

Making a Compost Heap

Every gardener serious about saving money will have a compost heap and/or bin. It's easy and cheap to recycle your own garden and kitchen waste effectively as compost.

There are as many different methods for building a compost heap as there are recipes for bolognaise sauce. Some methods require building the heap carefully and then leaving it; others require plenty of vigorous exercise on the part of the gardener as the pile needs to be turned often and regularly (rather like tossing a salad). Of course, you can build a compost heap by merely chucking everything into a pile indiscriminately. It may take longer, but it'll rot down sooner or later. Whichever construction method you choose, the essential ingredients remain the same: organic matter (and its carbon–nitrogen ratio, usually written C:N), microorganisms, water, and oxygen.

Organic matter includes lawn clippings, leaf litter, prunings (shredding them in a mulcher speeds the composting process considerably, and there are cheap ways of accessing mulchers—see p. 44–5), chook litter, hay, kitchen scraps, manure, paper, sawdust, straw and weeds.

Microorganisms find their own way into a heap eventually, but you can speed the composting process by layering small amounts of good garden topsoil through your heap, thereby 'seeding' with microorganisms.

Water is essential. The heap should be moist but not wet. You can add moisture by

> **C:N** refers to the proportion of dry, woody materials (high in carbon and low in nitrogen) to the proportion of green, meaty, high-nitrogen materials. High-nitrogen materials can usually be identified because they're high in energy and tend to be smelly when composting: kitchen scraps, dog poo, grass clippings and so on. High-carbon materials include twigs, sawdust and the leaves of deciduous trees. You need a balance of high-nitrogen and high-carbon materials for optimal compost breakdown—too many high-carbon materials and the heap takes ages to compost; too many high-nitrogen materials and you get a soggy, stinky mess that will have the neighbours complaining to the local Health Department.

including 'wet' ingredients (lawn clippings, kitchen scraps), or by sprinkling the heap with water as you build it.

Oxygen will be present in any heap that isn't excessively compacted. You can include coarse prunings and twigs through the heap or enclose it with open mesh or wire to maximise air flow.

A compost bay may be constructed of bricks, wire, stone, or corrugated iron; you can also use a pit (poor aeration may slow the composting process), or pile compost on the ground. The heap should be at least one cubic metre (preferably bigger, with a smaller surface area–volume ratio) to help heat build-up and retention during the composting process (a 'hot' heap kills many weed seeds and pathogens).

Like bolognaise sauce, your compost heap will comprise what you have to hand. Ideally you'll use a mixture of coarse and fine materials, those high in nitrogen (lush greens, manures, kitchen scraps) and low in nitrogen (woody materials like sawdust, prunings, and straw).

You'll get a feel for what works, and after a while you won't need a recipe but will throw things together as you do for bolognaise sauce.

A *Simple Composting Recipe That Works*

A simple recipe that works for me is as follows:

1. Over a period of weeks or months, chuck all prunings, weeds, leaves, and lawn clippings into an out-of-the-way corner. When a decent amount has accumulated (at least one cubic metre), it's time to build the heap.
2. Place a layer of coarse prunings or twigs in the base of a bay, container or pit. Top with a 10–20-centimetre layer of your accumulated organic matter. If it looks dry, I place a sprinkler at one side so that the spray evenly wets the material while I'm building the heap.
3. Throw in a few handfuls of high-nitrogen organic fertiliser (chicken manure, a few spadefuls of cow manure) or—if you have no access to organic fertilisers—a sprinkling of high-nitrogen chemical fertiliser (e.g. Complete D) over the organic matter. Urine isn't bad, either.
4. Sprinkle a spadeful of good garden soil over the organic matter.
5. Add another layer of organic matter and repeat from Step 3.
6. Use when ready (the compost will be moist, light, crumbly and more or less homogeneous).

Sprinkling lime, dolomite or wood ashes can speed the composting process but you'll lose more nitrogen in the form of gaseous ammonia. Decide whether you want compost quickly, or whether you'd prefer a more nutritious compost a bit later.

Don't be afraid to play around with the recipe. At worst, your heap will take an extra month or so to break down, or smell bad for a week. At best, you'll learn far more from your experiments than from following my instructions to the letter. After a while, you'll recognise what the heap needs and vary the proportions as necessary. You'll be able to tell when the heap is too wet or dry (in many areas of Australia you'll need to wet the heap during the dry months). You'll also get better at judging the best carbon to nitrogen ratio for optimum breakdown, so you'll add more chook manure or fertiliser to woody materials, and less or none to very green materials.

Bon appetit!

Making Compost in Bins

Compost produced in sealed drums or containers (usually bins) requires less oxygen than that required by open compost heaps. The composting process is known as an 'anaerobic system' because much of the breaking down is done by microorganisms that thrive in low-oxygen environments. You can buy specially made bins that are designed to maximise heat absorption, but an ordinary plastic garbage bin or large drum will do, and is much cheaper. Choose one with the most close-fitting lid you can find to minimise blowies and other unsavories getting in. Darker colours heat more quickly and speed the composting process. I recommend buying two bins so that you can use the second bin when the first is filled and 'cooking'.

It's not essential, but you may prefer to cut the bottom out of the bin and bury the lower edge a few centimetres. This helps with drainage and also lets soil microorganisms and, later, worms enter the compost to help it break down. Place the bin in a sunny spot for maximum heat absorption.

Because the bin is sealed, you can put in smelly kitchen scraps like vegetables and meat, as well as other materials (like dog and cat poo) that you wouldn't want on an open compost heap attracting rats, dogs, cats, blowies and small children. And because the ingredients generally have a low carbon to nitrogen ratio, the resulting compost is very rich, to be used almost more like a fertiliser than a compost.

You'll be amazed at how much material fits into such a compost bin, because the material breaks down as you add to it. Throw in a

TIP

You can put pet faeces in home garden closed compost systems, but commonsense is important to prevent the spread of disease. Don't compost faeces from cats less than a year old (toxoplasmosis is spread in their faeces), and don't use composted cat or dog faeces where it will come into contact with edible crops (e.g. in the vegetable garden). Compost thoroughly (at least a year) before use, and don't apply to areas you regularly work in with bare hands. Observe basic hygiene.

few handfuls of soil every now and then, especially if it looks too wet (overly wet bins smell especially bad). A light dusting of dolomite promotes breakdown and helps minimise smells, too.

Once the bin is almost full, cover with a few centimetres of good garden soil, leaving a 5–10-centimetre space between it and the lid. Close up the bin and leave it to stew for one to four months, depending on the ingredients, size of the bin, and temperature. When the compost is ready, it will have no offensive smell, feel pleasantly crumbly, and look homogeneously dark brown.

Green Manures

Green manuring is a clever and cheap method of fertilising whereby you sow an area with a quick-growing crop, usually in winter, then dig in the green manure just as it's coming into flower and when the soil is beginning to warm up. All you need to buy is the seed.

You can use a range of plants including barley, mustard, oats, rye, and wheat. Legumes (alfalfa, clover, field peas, tick beans, and vetches) are particularly good because they 'fix' nitrogen, so that when you dig in the green manure there's a high amount of nitrogen for your next crop. Sow legumes alone or in combination with non-leguminous crops. It's even better if you add a sprinkling of blood and bone or chook manure at the time of digging in the green manure; this hurries along decomposition. Green manuring is simple to do and complications are likely to occur only if you try to plant your crop too soon after digging in the manure, when the soil may be temporarily nitrogen deficient. Wait a few weeks (more in cold weather) before planting your next crop.

Mulches

Generally, mulches comprise coarse materials that are not mixed into the soil but placed in a layer on top of it. They range from the commonly used bark and wood chips to carpet underlay, grass clippings, hay/straw, newspaper, packing materials, pine needles, sawdust, seaweed, shells/hulls, and more.

Mulches promote healthy plants by:
1. conserving soil moisture (the layer prevents evaporation)
2. maintaining even temperatures around the plants' roots
3. encouraging worm activity closer to the soil surface
4. encouraging soil microorganisms
5. providing plant nutrients as they gradually break down
6. suppressing weeds

In some regions you may wish to mulch with non-organic materials, especially if it's to be a 'plant and forget' site with little further maintenance (don't use gravel or scoria if you plan to replant the bed regularly, as this mulch mixes with soil and can make it difficult to work). Gravel and stones are excellent for maintaining soil temperatures and reducing evaporation, but don't, of course, supply plant nutrients, at least not for tens of thousands of years.

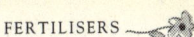

Mulches, especially finer, less woody materials, may be mixed into the soil, but this should be done well before planting time because the breakdown process of fresh organic matter depletes the soil of nitrogen. Avoid mixing in coarse, woody materials that will be very slow to break down.

Soluble Foliar Fertilisers

Organic foliar fertilisers (e.g. fish emulsion, seaweed extract), like their chemical equivalents, are quick-acting and highly effective. Unfortunately, they're also relatively expensive, and their high-nitrogen content promotes the kind of lush leaf growth that insect pests love. Use them as a supplement, not a staple, and not at all if money is tight.

Chemical Fertilisers

Chemical fertilisers may, at first glance, seem more expensive than organic ones, but this is because they are far more concentrated. When you analyse concentrations of active ingredients, chemical fertilisers are usually many times cheaper than their organic equivalent. You use only a handful of Complete D, but a few bucketfuls of cow manure. Because of the concentrated nature of chemical fertilisers in powder form, **most should be watered in immediately after application so as not to burn plant roots**. It's not a bad idea to do this for organic fertilisers as well, especially 'hot' ones like chicken and pigeon manure .

Chemical fertilisers also have the advantage of convenience. One tablespoon of slow-release fertiliser granules in a pot plant will last three, six or twelve months (depending on the brand).

Beware, though, of the 'fm' content of many fertilisers. 'Fm' stands for 'fine materials'—inactive rubbish—present in the bag along with the active ingredients. Note, too, that acetate-soluble forms of nutrients

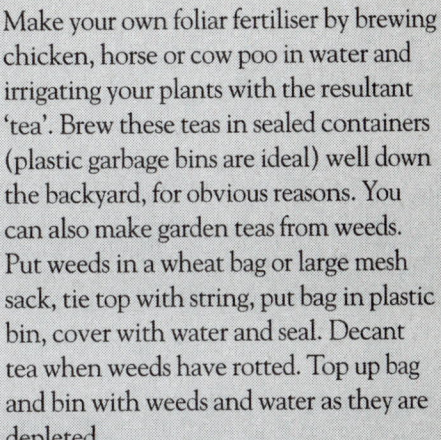

TIP

Brew Your Own Organic Foliar Fertilisers
Make your own foliar fertiliser by brewing chicken, horse or cow poo in water and irrigating your plants with the resultant 'tea'. Brew these teas in sealed containers (plastic garbage bins are ideal) well down the backyard, for obvious reasons. You can also make garden teas from weeds. Put weeds in a wheat bag or large mesh sack, tie top with string, put bag in plastic bin, cover with water and seal. Decant tea when weeds have rotted. Top up bag and bin with weeds and water as they are depleted.

are generally unavailable to plants, so figures for the total amount of nutrient can be misleading.

There are so many chemical fertilisers on the market that it's possible here to list only the main categories (see Appendix 7 for more).

Balanced Chemical Fertiliers

Slow-release Granules
Slow-release granules (e.g. Osmocote™, Nutricote™) are generally good value for money, especially if you buy home-brand ones (some garden centres stock these in a large bin and you buy by weight or volume). They're available as balanced fertilisers, as well as in different N:P:K ratios to promote flower, fruit, or leaf growth, or to suit different kinds of plants (Australian natives, vegetables, ferns and indoor plants).

Foliar Fertilisers
Foliar fertilisers (e.g. Thrive™ and Phostrogen™) are usually relatively expensive, but have the advantage of very quick results because they're absorbed so readily.

Avoid relying solely on foliar fertilisers because they tend to promote soft, lush growth that's particularly appealing to insect pests. Some brands designed to promote flowering are unbeatable for quick effects, but avoid foliar fertilisers if you want to save money. You should always use foliar fertilisers in mild weather because they can burn leaves in excessively hot or windy conditions. And you'll get best results if you spray in the late afternoon or early evening. *Never* make solutions stronger than the recommended dose because you can scorch the leaves permanently.

Soluble Chemical Fertilisers

Most balanced chemical fertilisers (e.g. Complete D, Complete Mineral Mix) are highly soluble, so are available to the plant like a quick hit of sugar, rather than a slow digestion and release of carbohydrate, for quick results (e.g. to green up lawns). Unlike slow-release fertilisers, soluble chemical fertilisers should therefore be applied in small doses and often, to avoid overdosing your plants.

Soluble chemical fertilisers with different N:P:K ratios and acidity levels are available to meet the needs of different plants (citrus, camellias, lawns, orchids, African violets, tomatoes, bulbs, and almost every popularly grown plant group you can think of). They're generally relatively expensive. You may find it cheaper to buy a home-brand general-purpose balanced fertiliser, and top up with whichever primary nutrient it is that the plant requires in greater amounts, especially if it's nitrogen, which you can add via compost or animal manure.

Complete D is a classic, balanced, all-purpose general fertiliser containing about 8 per cent nitrogen and potassium, and 3.5 per cent phosphorus. It also contains trace elements.

Complete Mineral Mix is another popular chemical fertiliser, high in nitrogen (about 10 per cent), lower in potassium (5 per cent), and with just a touch of phosphorus (about 1.5 per cent), as well as trace elements.

Specific Chemical Fertilisers

Most specific chemical fertilisers are soluble and therefore quick-acting.

Nitrogenous Fertilisers

Nitrogenous fertilisers (e.g. ammonium sulphate, ammonium nitrate) are high in nitrogen and provide value for money if that's what your soil and plants need. Most should nevertheless be seen as 'quick-fix' solutions rather than as long-term soil improvers because, although they're readily available, they won't last long in the soil and their concentrated and unbalanced nature means they can burn plant roots and damage soil life. Many supply only nitrogen:

- calcium nitrate (15.5 per cent N)
- nitrate of soda (16 per cent N)
- nitrogen solutions (18–41 per cent N)
- ammonium sulphate (20.5 per cent N)
- ammonium nitrate (33 per cent N)
- anhydrous ammonia (82 per cent N)

Others supply a combination of nitrogen and phosphorus:

- ammonium phosphate (11 per cent N, 48.8 per cent P)
- ammonium phosphate–sulphate (16 per cent N, 20 per cent P)
- diammonium phosphate (21 per cent N, 53 per cent P)

And another group contains a combination of nitrogen and potassium:

- nitrate of potash (13 per cent N, 44 per cent K)
- nitrate of soda–potash (15 per cent N, 14 per cent K)

Urea
Urea is an organic compound since it contains organic carbon, but in the form in

which it is purchased in the shop it is not a natural organic. It is extremely high in nitrogen (42–46 per cent), so a value-for-money way to buy if that's all you need, but it doesn't contain phosphorus or potassium. Use it with care—it's very easy to burn plants with this highly concentrated fertiliser.

Note: **Urine** is sterile, high in nitrogen, and has been used as a fertiliser for centuries. I'll say no more, except that you should use your imagination and your commonsense (Health Department regulations apply to the disposal and use of human waste).

Phosphate

Seen for a long time as the salvation of Australian farmers, superphosphate (16–20 per cent P) provided a relatively cheap source of this nutrient in our phosphorus-poor soils. Many proponents of organic farming assert that heavy and sustained use of superphosphate has damaged soil structure on farms around Australia, and this may well be true in marginal areas or where heavy use has

destroyed soil microflora. You won't have this trouble if you use phosphoric fertilisers as a supplement, rather than a staple (you should rely on compost to provide the staple). Other chemical phosphoric fertilisers include:

- rock phosphate (33 per cent total P)
- double superphosphate (42–47 per cent P)
- phosphoric acid solution (52 per cent P)
- calcium metaphosphate (63 per cent P)

Unless you have a severe and identified phosphorus deficiency in your garden, I'd recommend against using such potent specific fertilisers, because it's all too easy to upset the nutrient balance of your soil.

Potash (Potassium)

Fertilisers high in potassium include:

- Kainit (12–16 per cent K)
- sulphate of potash–magnesia (21–22 per cent K)
- manure salts (20–30 per cent K)
- sulphate of potash (48–52 per cent K)
- muriate of potash (48–62 per cent K)

CHAPTER 8

Water

Unless you're lucky enough to have a bore or enormous water tank in your backyard, chances are you'll be paying for your water—and with state water authorities increasingly introducing user-pays systems, you can be up for big bucks. The bucks will be even bigger if you live in temperate areas with high temperatures and low rainfall in summer. Still, even if you're not paying for water, you should aim at conserving it: water is a precious resource and indiscriminate use is not only wasteful but can eventually build up salinity in the soil. There are several strategies you can use to save water in your own garden. The more strategies you incorporate, the less you'll spend, if not initially, then in the long run.

Careful Plant Selection

Consider Climate
Certain plants are more drought-tolerant than others, and you should consider selecting plants for this reason as well as aesthetics if you live in a dry area. This is not to say that your garden should comprise only cacti, succulents and arid-zone natives ... but you'll save a lot of money by avoiding notoriously sensitive species such as ferns, fuchsias and hydrangeas.

Avoid Voracious Roots
If you want a lush understorey of shrubs, you should also avoid planting trees with particularly voracious root systems. Pines, willows and most eucalypts outcompete understorey plantings, and no matter how much water you pour on, you'll be struggling to keep the shrubs looking good (the trees, on the other hand, will definitely flourish!).

Choose Hardy Plants
Nor need your garden comprise only those rather grey and shrivelled-looking arid-zone native species: many exotic plants are surprisingly hardy, especially once they're established. Roses, lavenders, photinias, viburnums, escallonias, coprosmas, and agapanthus may look a little scorched at the end of the dry season but will survive year after year (see Dought-tolerant Plants on p. 83).

Avoid Lawns
Lawns need an enormous amount of water, and the best way to save money is to omit one from your garden design altogether (see p. 66 for alternative groundcovers), or to minimise its size. However, if you must have grass, choose one of the drought-tolerant blends that survive on a fraction of the irrigation of conventional blends. To take full advantage

Drought-tolerant Plants

Acacia (many spp.)
Acanthus spinosus (Bear's Breeches)
Agapanthus umbellatus
Alyogyne huegelii (Blue Hibiscus)
Anigozanthos flavidus (Kangaroo Paw)
Aptenia cordifolia
Atriplex spp. (saltbushes)
Banksia (many spp.)
Callistemon (many spp.)
Ceanothus spp.
Cistus spp. (rock roses)
Cotoneaster horizontalis
Coprosma kirkii (Coprosma)
C. kirkii 'Variegata' (Variegated Coprosma)
Echium fastuosum (Pride of Madeira)
Enchylaena tomentosa (Ruby Saltbush)
Eremophila spp. (emu bushes)
Erigeron karvinskianus
Eucalyptus (many spp.)
× Fatshedera lizei
Gamolepis chrysanthemoides
Hakea (many spp.)
Hebe (many spp.)
Hedera helix (English Ivy)
Helleborus corsicus (Winter Rose)
H. orientalis (Lenten Rose)
Hypericum calycinum
Kniphofia uvaria (Red Hot Poker)
Lavandula × allardi (Mitcham Lavender), L. stoechas (Italian Lavender), L. stoechas subsp. pedunculata (Spanish Lavender)
Leonotus leonuris (Lion's Ear)
Leucophyta brownii (Cushion Bush)
Melaleuca spp. (honey myrtles)
Nerine bowdenii (Nerine)
Phlomis fruticosa (Jerusalem Sage)
Rosa spp. (roses)
Rosmarinus officinalis (Rosemary)
Santolina chamaecyparissus (Cotton Lavender)
Sedum (many spp.)
Sempervivum (many spp.)
Stachys byzantina (Lamb's Ears)
Strelitzia reginae (Bird of Paradise)
Teucrium marum (Cat Thyme)
Vinca major 'Variegata' (Variegated Periwinkle)
Watsonia borbonica (Pink Watsonia)
Xanthorrhoea australis (Grass Tree)

of such blends you should prepare the soil correctly so the roots can grow deep enough to survive dry times. You'll need to rotary hoe, use quality soil (or improve what you have), and ensure drainage is good; you should also maintain soil porosity by annual coring.

For a coarser effect, you can choose the tough but potentially invasive buffalo or kikuyu grasses, but first ensure your lawn edging is effective or these grasses will take over your garden beds.

Careful Garden Design

Windbreaks

An enormous amount of water is lost from plant leaves as transpiration, and you can significantly reduce this loss by installing windbreaks around the boundaries of your property and around individual beds. Perimeter breaks have the added benefit of privacy screening, but should you prefer to maintain a view, a more open windbreak that slows (rather than stops) air movement will help as well.

On-site Retention Ponds

You can also incorporate an unlined pond that catches roof run-off, rather than allowing it to flow straight into the street. Such back-

Transpiration is the loss of water vapour to the atmosphere through openings in the leaves of plants. Large, soft leaves with a thin cuticle (e.g. hydrangea leaves) transpire more water than do small, thick or hairy leaves (e.g. saltbush leaves) in the same conditions.

yard retention basins not only provide water for surrounding trees, but also add humidity to the immediate area, allowing you to grow a wider range of plants. Because such ponds are unlined, the water soaks away relatively quickly, and mosquitoes are unlikely to be a problem except in impermeable clay soils.

Water in retention ponds will not stagnate if it drains away quickly; in areas where water is retained for longer, you can oxygenate it by planting the pond with sedges and other species that tolerate wetting and drying.

If adopted widely in urban environments, such basins are of enormous environmental benefit because they reduce the amount of stormwater flowing into our seas.

Contour Garden Beds

Contouring garden beds to retain water, rather than shedding it, is a highly effective technique. Raised garden beds can be shaped with a shallow depression or hollow on the top, which then catches and holds water from heavy showers while still providing drainage and preventing waterlogging.

Effective Irrigation Practices

Hand-watering garden beds is a popular but usually rather pointless gardening activity because it gives only the illusion of providing water: foliage and soil surfaces are wetted, but the rootzone remains dry. In fact, regular shallow watering can actually *increase* the chance of plant death during dry spells; the plant's roots remain at the surface of the soil (where the water is), rather than growing deep. Even one missed watering or period without rain will then be enough for the surface to dry out and kill such shallow-rooted plants.

Water Deeply

Watering is therefore much more effective if done less frequently, but deeply—once a week for one hour or four, rather than daily

for ten minutes. Rate of application should be such that there is no run-off (and wastage), and varies with soil type (clay soils need a slower rate than sandy ones). Obviously, you'll need to apply water more slowly on sloping sites, too.

Conversely, very fine micro-jet sprays apply water slowly, but watch it's not *too* slow: you may well be losing 40 per cent or more to the slightest breeze! The droplets should be large enough to actually fall, unless you aim to increase humidity in a shadehouse or under a pergola.

The best way to identify the effectiveness of a particular watering regime is to *look*. Many books advocate placing an ice-cream container under the sprinkler to measure application; even better, I've found, is to actually dig down into the soil after one hour, two hours, three hours and longer if necessary to see how deep the water has penetrated. This should be your guide.

Don't Be Misled by Wilting Foliage

Don't be misled by wilting foliage in hot spells. In very hot, dry and/or windy weather, it's quite possible for some plants (notably broad-leaved ones such as hydrangeas) to wilt drastically, even though the soil around the roots is moist. This is because the plant is losing water through its leaves faster than it can suck up water through its roots. If you start throwing water around while the leaves are drooping and the sun is high, the effect is similar to that of steaming spinach. Most plants recover spontaneously when the sun goes down or the wind drops. If you can't bear to see your plant suffer, shade it with cloth or—for smaller plants—a few leafy twigs or branches inserted in the ground. If the plant wilts even when well-established and on a regular basis, then consider moving it to a more sheltered position, giving it to a friend, or throwing it onto the compost heap. Life is too short to spend hours draping shadecloth over bushes.

Water at the Right Time of Day

In temperate areas, avoid watering in the sunniest time of the day. You'll lose less through evaporation if you wait until evening or night, and in areas where the water supply is high in salt, you'll avoid leaf burn. The exception to evening watering is in the vegetable garden and on lawn, which are susceptible to fungal diseases: these are best watered early in the morning, so the rising sun dries the leaves.

Furrow Irrigation

You can also reduce both fungal disease and water costs in vegie gardens by using furrow irrigation (just spread mulch straight over the furrow—the water will fill the furrow and soak down regardless). An energy dissipator is a hose attatchment that reduces the velocity of the water, so that when you lay the hose in the furrow and turn on the tap full bore, the water will flow, not squirt. This means that the water comes out quickly enough to fill the entire furrow (too slow, and it just dribbles out to wet one end) without gouging out soil or forcing the hose to swish about. You can easily make your own energy dissipator by wiring a sock, sponge or perforated aluminium can to the end of your hose, or you can buy a Water Wonder™ for about $5 (including postage and handling) from:

Eco Products
(Peter Bennett's Organic Garden and
Farm Service and Supply Centre)
2 L'Estrange St
Glenside 5065
South Australia
Tel. (08) 8379 7999

Improving Soil

Improving soil (especially sand, but also clay) with **organic matter** also saves on water costs. Why? Because humus not only improves fertility by providing nutrients but also acts as a sponge, increasing the water-holding capacity of the soil: you'll need to apply less water, less often. To save water, humus should be dug through the soil, rather than being spread on the surface like a mulch. For more details on soil improvement, see Chapters 5 and 7.

The high-nutrient, low bulk 'manures' like chicken, pigeon, dynamic lifters and anaerobic composts (produced in sealed bins) are excellent fertilisers but less effective as sponges. Avoid them if your main aim is to improve the water-holding capacity (and not the fertility) of the soil. However, if you have access to high-nutrient manures, you can mix them with fresh sawdust, straw or any bulky, low-nutrient organic matter, and compost them together to produce an excellent soil additive.

Generally, though, choose compost and *bulky* manures to save water costs: horse, cow, sheep and especially spadefuls, bucketfuls, *barrowfuls* from the compost heap.

Composted lawn clippings work well too, in both sandy and clay soils (but don't dig in large amounts of *fresh* lawn clippings, because they'll temporarily deplete the soil of nitrogen). Composted grass clippings are ready to dig in when they look dryish and brown, and feel light and crumbly.

Compressed peat moss is expensive but especially effective for sandy soil (it holds many times its weight in water, and lasts longer than most other composts). It's also very acid and will be most beneficial on neutral to alkaline soils.

Mushroom compost (a combination of rotted straw and horse manure) is very alkaline and is better on acid soils.

You can also buy **commercial soil-wetting preparations** for heavy clays and hydrophobic sands. These preparations are generally diluted in the watering can and sprinkled onto the soil surface. They work by improving water penetration, so you lose less water (and money) through run-off. Remember that all wetting agents are very toxic to frogs.

Gypsum is an excellent and cheap additive for clay soils. It acts on the clay particles, making them form tiny clumps. The resulting soil texture is more crumbly and friable, allowing water to penetrate more easily.

For pots and tubs, **water-holding crystals** are effective, but they're too expensive to incorporate into garden beds.

Mulching

Mulches are probably the single most effective water-saving technique for temperate areas of Australia. Mulches work by protecting the soil surface from the sun and air movement, thereby reducing evaporation and maintaining the soil temperature at a consistent level. They also hold water themselves, and slow the speed at which water flows over the surface of soil on sloping sites, thereby increasing penetration and reducing run-off.

Numerous mulches are available, from very cheap to expensive (see pp. 48, 57), but if your primary aim is to conserve water then the mulch you choose should be reasonably coarse. Very fine mulches placed on the soil surface tend to hold water and encourage roots to grow up into them, which is not the effect you want. Better to choose coarser mulches, such as straw, bark chips or hulls. These mulches won't absorb water, but let moisture run through them to soak into the ground beneath (and hence encourage the roots to grow down). At the same time, they'll reduce evaporation from the soil surface to almost zero, especially in windy areas.

When you're watering, be sure to choose a sprinkler head that produces water droplets heavy enough to penetrate the mulch. With any newly applied mulch, it's best to check that you're wetting the soil, and not just the mulch.

CHAPTER 9

Good Design and Planning

The task of designing a garden from scratch is a daunting prospect for most new gardeners. Where to start? When to start? What to do? Luckily, even if you're the most cash-strapped and inexperienced of gardeners, there are choices available, provided you're prepared to spend time, elbow grease and brain power to achieve the results you want.

On the other hand, although paying for good design may seem contradictory in a book about saving money in the garden, don't be misled: bad design is much more expensive than anything you'll pay a professional.

How Good Design and Planning Save You Money

Good design and planning can save you hundreds, even thousands, of dollars in the long term by *preventing* costly mistakes.

Protecting Foundations

That Moreton Bay fig tree you naively planted a few metres from the house will eventually crack foundations and walls with its massive root system. Even if you remove it before the damage is done to your house, it's too late for your wallet—tree-loppers can charge thousands of dollars to cut down established trees.

Preventing Drainage Problems

Drainage problems around structures are generally caused or exacerbated by poor planning, and removed or ameliorated by good design. Slopes that direct water towards foundations of buildings may not cause rising damp in modern houses with damp-coursing, but certainly contribute to a musty atmosphere that is unpleasant to live in and that begs frequent and costly coats of paint. In sheds and carports, excess water rots timbers and damages walls and floors.

Reducing Heating/Cooling Costs

Just as good design principles relating to house orientation, insulation, verandahs, and window size and placement save thousands of dollars in heating and cooling costs during a lifetime, the garden you design can directly affect long-term expenses. A strategically placed deciduous tree shades the house in summer and reduces cooling costs, yet lets the sunlight and warmth in during winter. A dense evergreen tree, on the other hand, cuts cooling costs in summer, but may actually *increase* heating costs in winter if it prevents low sunlight reaching the windows.

Reducing Maintenance Costs

Good design and planning reduce maintenance costs. It may be tempting to choose

that vigorous climber (ivy is a horribly familiar example) to provide extra-quick cover,
but you'll be cursing when you have to prune
it each fortnight to stop it strangling your
trees or lifting the tiles from your roof.
Vigorous climbers often overwhelm all but
the strongest of structures: I've seen wisteria
make a steel and corrugated fence collapse,
and a glory vine split apart a pergola.

Reducing Irrigation Costs

Good design saves you money on water, especially in temperate areas of Australia. The
shape and slope of garden beds, and the posi-
tioning of windbreaks and structures, impact
enormously on evaporation and transpiration
(Chapter 8 describes this in more detail).

Increasing the Value of Your House

Good design increases the resale value of
your house by up to 20 per cent; a beautiful
garden is the first and last thing a buyer sees
when viewing your property, and both
impressions are powerful ones.

Improving Lifestyle

You'll be looking at your garden, and living
in it, for days, weeks, years, even decades of
your life. A beautiful garden will save you
heartache and enrich your life in ways that,
though they can't be measured in dollar
terms, are of equal value. Or more.

When to Plan

The earlier in the development phase you
can incorporate careful garden planning, the
more money you'll save. The ideal time is
before the house is built, not afterwards.
Though few of us are in that lucky situation,
grab the chance, if you have it, to ensure that
topsoil is retained (much cheaper than
buying in soil or compost later). Plan earthworks for footings or cuts into hillsides to
allow for lawns and garden beds as well as the
house proper: far cheaper to do it in one hit

than to hire machinery later. Heavy machinery brought in later is likely to compact existing lawns and crush garden plants (in fact,
there may not even be access for machines!).
And good planning means you won't be
ripping up lawn to install paving or vice
versa.

If you're moving into an established home,
plan carefully *before* implementing any major
projects or changes.

Landscaping and Design Choices Available

There is a range of design options available,
ranging from expensive to free. Not surprisingly, conventional landscaping businesses
cater to gardeners with money (sometimes,
lots of money—I've seen a walled suburban
back garden that cost more to design and
construct than the house in which I live!).
Other landscapers are cheaper, but how do
you recognise the one who will best suit you?
What do you look for?

I suggest that there are five design options
available to you, though of course a spectrum
exists with overlapping costs, depending on
how you decide to go about things.

1. Garden plan by a landscape architect
2. Garden plan by a landscape contractor
   or designer
3. Garden consultation by a landscape
   architect, contractor or designer
4. Suggestions from friends experienced in
   gardening
5. Drawing your own plan

The free alternatives (that is, options 4
and 5) are excellent but depend on the
quality of advice you're given. Do you have
friends who are experienced enough to give
you sound advice? Do you have, or can you
gain, sufficient knowledge to have a go yourself? Read this chapter, plus other books on
garden design, and decide.

If you're considering going down the path

Tools and Equipment

My favourite weeding tool: a plasterer's knife. It's not as large and unwieldy as a hand fork or trowel, but stronger than a kitchen knife.

Visit an Independent Living Centre to see some great products for those with mobility problems, arthritis or other conditions that make gardening difficult. Most are lightweight and have special ratchet actions; others are adapted to allow one-handed operation. Many have interchangeable ends so you need buy only one handle.

Landscaping Materials

Most local garden centres have a range of soils, mulches, composts, bedding materials and more. Most centres will also mix media to your specification (e.g. 75 per cent sandy loam, 25 per cent compost).

Ask your local lawn-cutters and tree-loppers to give you their clippings. Lawn clippings and mulched tree prunings make beautiful mulch and compost, though you'll need space and time for them to break down. Deep chicken litter will speed the composting process.

Pest Control

There's a huge range of pesticides available. The ones on the right are generally classified as 'organic', the ones on the left 'chemical'. In the centre is a range of glyphosate herbicides—the same active ingredient but different amounts, concentrations and prices. Compare to determine best value for money.

Bugle weed (here, *Ajuga reptans* 'Jungle Beauty') spreads to create a vigorous weed-suppressing groundcover in semishaded areas.

The red-tinted foliage of *Polygonum capitatum* makes a dense, vigorous weed-suppressing groundcover in sunny areas.

Naturalising annuals and perennials will eventually compete with most weeds after a few years of selective weeding. Here, Love-in-the-Mist (*Nigella damascena*), Heartsease (*Viola tricolor*), Pink Yarrow (*Achillea* sp.) and Feverfew (*Chrysanthemum parthenium*).

In mild temperate climates, aquilegias will eventually compete with weeds after a few years of selective weeding.

Hardy yellow *Gazania* and *Arctotis* are dense, drought-resistant groundcovers that effectively smother weeds and will spread (but not invasively) to cover large areas.

Fertilisers

There's a huge range of fertilisers available. Organic fertilisers are generally bulkier and more expensive but softer on the environment. Chemical fertilisers may be general or specific (to correct deficiencies or to boost flowers or fruit). They may be quick-acting, slow-release, or foliar.

Closed composting systems, such as this Gedye™ bin, are ideal for high-nitrogen materials that attract flies, rats and other nasties when they are put on an open heap.

Save water by spreading mulch (here, pea straw).

Plants That Save on Water Costs

Winter Rose (*Helleborus orientalis*) is a hardy herbaceous perennial that will tolerate dry shade. In more moist conditions and in good soil, it will naturalise.

Callistemons (here, C. 'Western Glory') are hardy Australian natives. Once established, many will survive temperate summers without any extra water.

Cistus are hardy shrubs for dry temperate climates. Here, C. *populifolius*

Good Design and Planning

This is an informal 'cottage' garden. Note the flowing lines, with mixed perennials spilling from the beds, and see too how this garden complements the stone house.

Another informal garden, but more formally planted than the one above. Note the mass plantings of tulips which unify the garden.

For environmental reasons I discourage the use of moss rocks when used purely for decorative reasons. Here, however, I confess I was impressed by the clever and highly practical placement of the rocks to retain a steep sloping block without formal terracing.

Pockets of soil allow for the planting of plenty of small annuals and perennials between the rocks.

Texture is an important element in garden design. Here, pebbles, stone and wood contrast with the different shapes and sizes of the foliage.

Texture provides aesthetic interest in the garden: choosing plants that are the same size, shape and colour results in a boring garden. Choose variety for visual effect.

More complementary colours: mauve Canterbury Bells and pink rose blooms look terrific with the silver foliage of *Centaurea cineraria*.

Plan structures carefully. Add an arch to a gate to form a lych-gate and use as a structure on which to grow climbing roses.

Lilies and *Caltha palustris* adorn a small water feature.

TIP

What's in a Name?
A **landscape architect** is
trained in a degree course at a university. The course covers the outdoor
environment in its broadest sense, with
an emphasis on design and planning.
For major works, the landscape architect may be head consultant or part of a
team. Landscape architects hire landscape contractors to implement the
plan.

A **landscape contractor** must hold a
builder's licence (or equivalent, depending on their home State), and tenders
for and constructs work specified by the
landscape architect, or contracts direct
to the garden owner. Landscape contractors may or may not have additional
management, technical and horticultural qualifications; experience counts
for a lot, too. Most provide detailed
plans and fixed quotes if requested.

A **garden designer** is a contractor
with particularly strong horticultural
and garden design experience and/or
qualifications (certificate or diploma).
Garden designers have plenty of practical knowledge about plants and their
growing requirements, and most provide
detailed plans and fixed quotes if
requested.

TIP

The three main elements
which determine the quality of
a landscaper is their expertise in
- design
- construction
- horticulture

The person you hire may not be highly
skilled in all three areas, but this isn't a
problem provided they subcontract
someone with the expertise they themselves lack.

(sorry) of paying someone to design your
garden for you (that is, options 1, 2 or 3), it's
important that you view their work, and
absolutely essential if you want them to
implement the design. All established and
reputable landscapers, be they architects,
designers or gardeners, should be able to
present for your inspection a folio of their
work comprising plans and photographs of
completed gardens they've designed. Photos
provide a good indication as to whether your

ideas mesh (good landscapers work with your
ideas, rather than impose their own on you)
and whether you like their work. It's worth
viewing a few of the landscapers' gardens a
few years after establishment as well their
newer gardens, because design (as well as
maintenance, of course) influences whether
a garden improves or deteriorates with time.

Landscapers usually buy plants from nurseries at wholesale prices, and charge them to
you at retail prices. If you have a cheap
source of plants, or can propagate your own
(see Chapter 3), you may be able to use their
list while supplying your own stock.

Be aware that charges vary enormously,
not only between but within categories of
landscape architect, landscape designer and
landscape contractor. A well-known or
award-winning landscape designer may
charge as much or more than a landscape
architect. And formal qualifications on their
own don't guarantee a good job. My belief is
that an experienced landscaper with natural
flair can create a more pleasing garden than
someone with qualifications but no flair.

As a final consideration, put the cost of a
landscape plan into perspective. Measure it
against the price of your house, your furnishings and floor coverings—doesn't the
amount of time you'll spend relaxing, recreating, working in or just looking at the

garden warrant a little more expenditure than you initially set aside?

If dollars are still a real constraint, it's definitely best to implement a little bit at a time properly, rather than to do the lot half-heartedly. You'll only end up altering, and paying for, it later.

1. Garden Plan by a Landscape Architect

Only architects accredited by the Australian Institute of Landscape Architects (AILA) are legally permitted to call themselves 'landscape architects', but this has not prevented many unqualified designers from using the label. However, you can check credentials by contacting the AILA on freecall 1800 020 063.

A conventional landscape plan drawn by an architect is highly detailed, professionally drafted and to scale. It usually comes on a large sheet of fancy paper, and shrubs, paving etc. are often attractively coloured with pencil or wash. Drainage and slopes are marked, plants are listed and numbered (often in neat calligraphy), and costings are accurate to the dollar when the plan also acts as a quote.

Unfortunately, these plans are expensive, starting at about $800–1000 (some architects charge around 5 per cent of the project cost, which gives you some idea of the total amount you'll be up for). That's $800–1000 for a piece of paper (and ideas, of course) without a single shrub planted or brick laid. This is fine if you aim to hang the plan beside the Streeton on your lounge room wall, but a waste of money if you don't want to pay for such a detailed presentation.

Though perhaps that's putting it a little strongly. Gardens designed by professional architects are usually beautifully structured once established, and you can be reasonably confident that no nasty little design flaws will surface several years down the track. On the other hand, such plans are often expensive to implement, because they tend to include major earthworks with upper-end-of-the-market materials and plants (let's face it, if you spend $800–1000 for a drawing of the garden, you should reasonably expect to spend a helluva lot more for the garden itself!). Still, you can cut costs by telling the architect that you require minimal labour and cheap plants (e.g. trees in tubes, instead of two-metre-high advanced specimens).

Many plans are designed to be implemented in one fell swoop, so you're not only up for big bucks, but big bucks all at once (anywhere from a few thousand dollars to fifty thousand dollars). However, you can decide to have the work carried out by contractors or by yourself, over a period of five, ten, or even twenty years, thereby spreading the cost.

Architects only design the garden; they don't implement the plan but hire contractors to do the work, so you are up for extra dollars. Most landscape contractors and gardener designers, on the other hand, do the work themselves and cut out the middle person.

2. Garden Plan by a Landscape Contractor or Designer

A garden plan by a landscape contractor or design is usually (but not always) a lower-key affair, although a code of ethics has been devised by the Landscape Industry Association.

The plan you receive varies with the designer. It may or may not be as detailed as those produced by landscape architects, but it should be to scale and include suggestions and a plant list. Costings are provided and these may or may not comprise a firm quote, or be approximate (though obviously landscape gardeners provide firm quotes if you employ them to do the work).

Overall, a garden plan from a landscape contractor or designer is cheaper because you're not paying for the landscape architect's training and design (as opposed to gardening skill) or presentation of the plan (though some landscape gardeners do present beautiful plans, correspondingly priced). Rest assured that there's no reason a contractor's or designer's plan should be inferior to a landscape architect's plan; in fact, a garden designed by an experienced contractor may well be superior to one designed by an inexperienced landscape architect. And because all good landscape gardeners understand plant growth and requirements, their gardens may well comprise more appropriate plants than those of an architect who understands design and space, but who has spent relatively little time studying plants or plant biology.

Some designers and landscape gardeners 'waive' the cost of the plan if you subsequently contract them to implement the design—a good deal if you can find one who does this (beware, though, because the cost of the plan may still be built into the overheads of the project).

3. Garden Consultation by a Landscape Contractor, Architect or Designer

A garden consultation is cheaper again. The contractor visits the site, draws up a rough plan, and discusses ideas and possibilities with you. A consultation is often charged out per hour, and may cost less than $150.

A garden consultation may be the perfect solution if you're a new gardener with plenty of elbow grease, but just don't know where to start: it will give you basic information about your site (soil, drainage, aspect), appropriate plants and so on. You can also employ the contractor to implement his or her ideas for you (probably after drawing a more detailed plan), but of course this is more expensive. Not all landscape contractors provide these initial no-obligation consultations, so you

may need to shop around to find one who does.

Some contractors may agree to undertake the job with you, the client, acting as labourer/assistant. This is an attractive option because it not only saves you money but gives you a real 'ownership' of the work.

4. Suggestions from Friends Experienced in Gardening

Friends and relatives who know you, as well as being keen gardeners themselves, are sure to be of help, whether or not you decide to go further later and get a professional plan drawn. Because these friends know your tastes, they may well make suggestions that a stranger, no matter how highly trained, is less likely to come up with.

Most keen gardeners love talking plants and gardens. Almost without exception I've found them a wonderfully generous bunch. Perhaps it's the nurturing skills any successful gardener must develop if their garden is to thrive. Whatever it is, you're likely to gain not only ideas, but offers of cuttings, seeds, plants and old pots.

Invite your friend for lunch, have a few glasses of wine, take a stroll around what currently passes for a garden, and ask them for ideas. Don't spring it on them, though. Tell them when you issue the invitation that you're trying to develop ideas for your garden—ask to borrow any books they think might prove useful to you.

Of course, this method is cheap, but it's also far more personal. The end results will depend on the skills and perceptiveness of your friends, and the knowledge base supporting the advice they give you. Still, such advice is a great starting point. If you're smart enough, know enough about plants, and have a sufficiently developed aesthetic eye, you may well be able to go on and design your own garden from the suggestions you receive.

Ask your friends about potential problems with drainage and foundations. Do they have suggestions to save money on watering or heating/cooling costs? If they're unsure, can they suggest someone who has more specialised knowledge? If not, double-check drainage, and any other major structural earthworks, before you turn the first sod. Some local councils and government authorities require that you first get planning approval for structural work; in any case, to prevent expensive and/or fatal mistakes, you should check with government authorities to be sure you know the exact whereabouts of underground services (water, phone, electricity and sewers) on your property.

5. Drawing Your Own Plan

Self-education is the key to success here. Use all the resources listed in Chapter 1: courses, libraries, and botanic gardens. Visit as many gardens as you can in the Open Garden Scheme. Be nosy; ask questions. The owners are usually on hand to answer questions, and most are generous with their knowledge. Make notes of plant names, combinations, effects with paving, retaining walls, garden edges, furniture.

Consider potential problems with drainage, foundations, excessive or insufficient shading (or other choices that may affect heating/cooling costs), and think about how much you're prepared to spend on water (design of garden beds, plant and irrigation system selection will all affect water costs).

Many nurseries, especially the smaller ones, employ staff who are happy to help you with ideas and plant selection if you're buying lots. But be courteous. It is the height of rudeness to spend an hour with an assistant, jotting names and suggestions onto your own plan and clipboard, only to leave and buy your plants elsewhere. As a part-time nursery assistant myself, I can guarantee from experience that you will receive a less warm welcome when you return!

Some nurseries and garden centres test your soil for you to determine its pH (acidity/alkalinity) and its texture. This is useful if you need to buy soil conditioners or are looking at improving drainage by buying gravel, gypsum or agricultural pipe. And most gardening courses provide an opportunity to conduct your own soil tests on samples brought along to classes. For about $20 you can also buy your own easy-to-use soil pH test kit from larger nurseries and garden centres.

Browse through books and magazines that specialise in garden design: the more you've seen, the wider the range of choices available to you. One of the most difficult skills to master as a new gardener is the ability to visualise possibilities: the alternatives we see are frequently limited by what is already there, or not there. Don't be afraid to change things—consider removing an old tree if you don't like it. You want a cohesive structural theme; the garden need not be developed all at once, but the best ones always look as if they have been, with different areas flowing into each other. What you should avoid is a garden that expresses little more than which plants were on sale last week at the local hardware store!

Try to view your garden objectively—you should aim to retain features because you like them for what they are, and not because they're there. If it's an established garden, avoid incorporating the previous owner's design flaws.

Designing your own garden takes time, and you'll make the odd mistake, but your reward at the end will be a garden that is truly your own. Many landscape gardeners are good at most of their job but, in spite of this, exhibit a certain depressing sameness of plant selection and design, so that anyone peering over your fence will know you've employed someone to 'do' your garden. In Adelaide, the dead-giveaways include Golden Diosma, 'Iceberg' roses, moss rocks and pine bark (usually separately, but sometimes—rather amazingly—in combination). No doubt cities in other states have their own 'this is a landscaped garden' look. Avoid it.

Designing Your Own Garden: A Step-by-Step Guide

Everyone has their own way of going about designing their garden. Much depends on how clearly you can visualise what you want—not just existing features, but potential features and possibilities. The more gardens you visit, and the more books you read during Steps 1 and 2, the wider the buffet of choices you'll have when you sit down to draft ideas onto paper in Step 4.

If you're a new gardener, designing a garden from scratch may seem daunting, but it *is* manageable—yes, even fun!—when broken down into stages. You don't believe me? Read on.

When planning a kitchen, you think first of your lifestyle (who will be using the kitchen and how?). You decide on essentials like sink, stove, and fridge first, and these items will reflect your lifestyle (frequent entertaining, large family, or small budget). You then consider essentials to fit around those features, like cupboards, exhausts, or range hoods. Then you either add or leave space for those things you'd *like*, but which may or may not be added immediately—

microwave, dishwasher, or cook (I wish!). Last of all, you select paint colour, tiles, counter surfaces and floor covering.

First, become familiar with your site and find out as much relevant information as you can (see Chapter 1 on self-education). After that, sketch your ideas on paper. Go from the general to the specific: work out what you want in your garden, then where it should go (it's nothing more than a giant jigsaw puzzle!). Add details such as paving surfaces and plant species last. Going from the general to the specific means your garden will be a whole, integrated living space, incorporating everything you *need*, and leaving room for everything you'd *like*.

Treat the drawing stage as flexibly as possible—your plan is fluid until the first sod is turned (and even then you can change your mind, unless you've literally poured concrete). Play around with those ideas on paper for as long as possible to help you discover and explore new options. Try not to be limited by existing features—removing a single tree or tool shed may open up a whole range of possibilities that extend around the site in a domino effect (moving the tool shed means an entertaining area can go *there*, which means the chook shed can be moved further back, so the vegie patch can be closer to the back door, and the clothes line now fits ... and so on).

Step 1: Wait

The first step is easy: do nothing except *look*—at your own garden and other people's. Whether you've moved into a new house surrounded by building rubble, or into an established property, try to resist the potent temptation of putting your mark on the land and making changes straight away. Wait six months (a year if you can hold out that long), so you begin to get a feel for existing conditions. That path you thought ridiculous is, in fact, the best route from A to B, and

> **TIP**
>
> IF YOU'VE EVER DESIGNED OR ARRANGED A ROOM IN A HOUSE, YOU CAN DESIGN A GARDEN.

Understanding where the sun falls in your garden at different times of the year—where north, south, east and west lie—will help you enormously in the planning stage and will prevent expensive mistakes. In Australia, areas south of the house, especially on a south-facing slope, may be sunny in summer but heavily shaded throughout winter.

Why is this relevant? Nearly all vegetables need almost full sun to thrive. Other plants prefer shade (ferns may thrive south of the house and frizzle north of the house). A sunny patio area for winter will be useless if it's planned in summer but shaded in winter. Many plants prefer mild morning (easterly) sunlight, but won't tolerate the hot westerly afternoon sun. North-facing slopes warm up more quickly in early spring, and can be planted with (say) tomatoes earlier than can south-facing slopes or flat ground. Northern boundary fences may provide shade in hot regions, while southern boundary fences may radiate welcome warmth in cool regions.

Borrow a compass, or just get up early in the mornings and make a note of where the sun rises (check to see where it sets, too). What areas are shady or sunny? For how long? At what time(s) of the day? Don't forget, the sun will be lower in the sky in winter.

you use it constantly. The tree blocking the winter sunlight also blocks the view of your neighbour's swimming pool. The dead shrub isn't dead at all but merely deciduous. You'll become familiar with the seasons and where the sun falls in winter and summer; in spring you discover an area you thought bare becomes a blaze of daffodil bulbs you didn't even know were there.

Of course, if you're itching to do something—*anything!*—it's okay to start improving the soil, gathering compost, even putting in a small (possibly temporary) vegie patch. Unless drainage or structural problems threaten the integrity of your house (in which case these should become your first priority), it's best to hold off making any major, *expensive* changes.

Principles of Good Garden Design

There have been hundreds, if not thousands, of books written on this subject, but good design boils down to the fact that the garden must look good and work well for the people who are using it. Some general principles are as follows:

- Plan for use and users (who and what?).
- Use complementary or contrasting colors and textures (of foliage, stone, wood, etc.).
- Aim for structural cohesiveness (usually—but not always—a blend of trees, shrubs and groundcovers).
- Explore space, light and shape.
- Incorporate sensual stimuli (sight, sound, smell, texture).
- Use mass, repeat and multiple plantings, vistas, and focal points.

If you've read the preceding chapters and you're the owner of a new garden, you'll probably already have ideas you want to incorporate. See Appendix 1 for books on garden design.

Read lots of design books. Learn the principles of good design (see Tip on p. 102).

Step 2: List Your Needs

Your list of needs will be as individual as you are. It will reflect the site, your taste, family (size, age), lifestyle (habits, hobbies) and budget. You'll probably need a place to put the garbage bins, and an outdoor area to relax in (whether it be a tennis court, swimming pool or secluded patch of lawn). You'll probably also want a clothes line and utility area, but their size will reflect the size and makeup of your family, and how fastidious you are about clean clothes!

Don't be limited by convention if it doesn't suit your situation. Most people like a lawn, but that's no reason for you to have one too. My grandmother's front garden originally comprised garden beds surrounding a lawn but, as the years passed, the beds expanded and the lawn shrank until all that remained were grassed pathways winding between flower beds. At this point my grandmother acknowledged the inevitable, killed the last few blades of grass on the paths, and resurfaced with mulch.

Certain needs are common to almost all house owners, so make sure these are included in your plan (see below for options to consider). Decide what the major features and essentials of *your* garden will be, and list them.

Families vary enormously and so do their needs. The following list includes considerations you may wish to include immediately, leave room for, or defer indefinitely.

aviary
barbecue
basketball/netball ring
chicken coop/run
clothes line
compost bin(s)
compost heap(s)
cubbyhouse
cut flowers/flower garden

dog/pet run
garage
garbage bin site
gazebo/pergola/patio
glasshouse
lawn(s)
orchard
outdoor entertaining area
tennis court
private/secluded area
sandpit
shadehouse
shed
swimming pool
vegie garden/herb garden
water (pond, fountain)
woodshed

Some Things to Think About

Your garden is an area you'll live in. For it to be a comfortable, practical and aesthetically pleasing place, you should consider utility areas, areas for recreation and entertaining , and problem areas you'll need to tackle. Think also about privacy and climate, and what kind of structures, furniture and plants you'll want in you garden. Fortunately, you don't need to think about all these factors at once; instead, consider them one at a time and you'll build up a picture of what your ideal garden will be.

Utility Areas

Chook Run

Chook runs are great for saving money. Chooks recycle scraps into compost *and* eggs, but most runs are not particularly attractive. Are you the kind of person who likes them down the back out of sight, or do you prefer the convenience of having them near the back door? What about the smell? We sited our run against the back fence, but somehow I forgot I'd have to feed the chooks daily—I'd put them closer to the back door if I were redesigning my garden.

Clothes Line

Will you need a clothes line? If yes, how big? Can you get away with a retractable one? I like retractables because they're neat and disappear when not in use, so the area can double for entertaining or recreation. If you prefer a conventional hoist, you can buy a specially made fabric cover, which turns your hoist into a shady umbrella. Add a table and a few chairs and—presto!—instant outdoor eating area!

Where are sunny or potentially sunny areas of the garden? A sunny area obviously dries clothes faster, but if it's the only warm spot you may prefer, as we did, to put the vegie patch there.

If there's an existing clothes line, should it be moved? It's usually a simple matter to do this, and it opens up a large space for alternative uses.

Compost Heap

Where will you site the compost heap and compost bins (if you're serious about saving money, you'll have them)? A compost heap requires more room (say, three to six square metres), but won't accommodate too many kitchen scraps; an anaerobic bin (about 0.7 square metres) accommodates scraps but not bulky garden prunings. Unless you're *very* pressed for space, environmentally aware gardeners should try to find room for both.

Garbage Bins

Garbage bins may be hidden by wooden screens (often covered by climbers) in small alcoves. Think about convenience here, not just aesthetics—remember that last-minute rush to beat the garbage collector?

Garden Shed

Do you need a garden shed? Most home owners find them useful for tools, bikes, and all that stuff you don't really want to store inside the house. Think about size, too. My back garden has three sheds: one for wood, one for 'good stuff' and one for 'whatever can't be stored elsewhere' (junk). That's three small sheds instead of one big one— easier to site on a smallish block. However, our woodshed is sited at the furthest corner of our (suburban) block, and, believe me, I curse its siting every winter.

Pet Housing

Will you have pets? Where will they be housed (kennel, chook run, hutch, aviary), or be allowed to roam? Will garden beds survive the onslaught? Our dog (then a puppy) initially roamed the entire backyard, but after six months the self-seeding annuals and perennials (forget-me-nots, aquilegias, foxgloves and Honesty) succumbed to trampling and failed to regrow. Rather than a sea of colour, our backyard resembled a moonscape. We didn't want to chain our dog, but compromised by fencing the yard in half lengthwise, and excluding the dog from the vegie patch.

Will nasty kitty surprises in the garden bother you? And what about kids (the most destructive kind are the two-legged ones)? You'll need to fence water features, of course, but if you have young children you'll have more peace of mind if you also barricade steep slopes.

Rainwater Tank

Will you add a rainwater tank, either immediately or later? Where will it go? Rainwater usually tastes better than mains water and you'll only need a small tank if it's just for drinking (we have a 500-litre one). On the other hand, if you have a large roof area, sufficient rainfall, and enough space for a big tank, natural rainfall may be enough to supply all your household and garden needs. In bushfire-prone regions, a tank and pump can save lives when mains pressure drops to zero. An on-site stormwater retention basin (in the form of an unlined pond) will also catch excess roof run-off, and will reduce watering costs (see Chapter 8); you'll need to fence the area to protect dogs and small children.

Recreation Areas and Entertaining

Entertaining Areas

Will you be entertaining frequently? If yes, you'll need a practical area that's worth spending a bit more on—view it as an extra living room, not just as garden. Think about whether you'll be entertaining formally or casually. Permanent tables, seating and a built-in barbecue plate are suited to frequent, more formal entertaining. You might want all-weather cover, too. If, on the other hand, you're more likely to have a few mates around only occasionally, with BYO drinks and chairs, an open area screened from the neighbours and street is all that's required— you can bring out the portable barbecue, Webber kettle, hibachi or folding picnic table and store them in the shed after the party.

How many people will you entertain, and at what time of year? This will determine how large the area will need to be, and whether a covered pergola or patio is more appropriate than a sunny back lawn or tree-shaded area of paving. If you'll do most of your food preparation inside, you might prefer an entertaining area close to the house.

Pool or Tennis Court

Will you at some stage want to incorporate a swimming pool or tennis court? Like a rain-water tank, a swimming pool has the potential to save lives in bushfire-prone areas.

Make sure that you leave space for such structures, even if you don't expect to install them for a decade. You can establish privacy screenings and shrubs in the meantime, but avoid planting large trees that will need to be removed. And remember not to block access with sheds, plants, walls or permanent fences, so that earth-moving equipment can get in to the area.

Play Areas

Do you need play areas for children? Are there places for a sandpit or cubbyhouse? If the kids are young, it's a good idea to site swings and play equipment so you can see them from (say) the kitchen window. For older children, you can erect a basketball ring on a wall beside a paved area or your driveway.

Kids love lawns, too, but have you considered the effects of a football in the vegetable garden? There's no easy answer to this problem, I'm afraid. Some dedicated gardeners ban balls completely, but my partner and I decided that the garden belonged to our children as well. So although the currant bushes in the backyard are off limits, the front flower bed became a bit of a sacrifice zone.

If there's room, most kids also appreciate a bit of wilderness in the garden, where they can have secret hideaways, forts, or just a bit of privacy.

Problem Areas

Areas with Excessive Root Competition

Are there areas choked with tree roots where competition makes establishing understorey plants difficult? You can remove the trees (this can be hugely expensive), but first consider using these areas for utility functions, chooks, entertaining, or any use that does not require the establishment of understorey plants.

Exposed Areas

Are there very hot, exposed areas? If you don't like the open look or feel of the site, you'll need to plant windbreaks or trees.

Shady Areas

Are there very shady areas? These are an asset in a hot climate, especially when planted with ferns and plants with large glossy leaves for a cool, lush effect. In a cold climate you may wish to add warmth and light by pruning trees or removing shrubs.

Steep Slopes

Are there very steep areas? A bare clay bank may, in fact, not be a problem at all. With terracing or the addition of retaining walls, and planted with trailing groundcovers, such banks make stunning garden features. Alternatively, you can use elbow grease (*lots of elbow grease*—I've done it and I know!) or contract a bobcat operator to recontour the area. Recontouring reshapes the bank, making it less steep and easier to stabilise with plants. The bobcat operator can also terrace the bank for you, or cut it back even further. Such recontouring often opens up a useful space. Before beginning any major earthworks, think about the effect it will have on access.

Wet or Boggy Areas

Are there boggy areas? Once again, you can work with nature and turn liability into asset: why not make a feature of the site as a pond or bog garden? Of course, if the boggy area threatens to damage existing or future structures like house footings, sheds, carports or swimming pools, you'll need to fix the problem. Some boggy areas can be dried through recontouring and directing water elsewhere; otherwise, you'll need to install agricultural pipes and/or surface drains to remove the water.

Privacy

Bad Neighbours

Do you have exceptionally nosy or unpleasant neighbours who require more than the usual discouragements? A dense hedge of climbing roses, bougainvilleas or needlebushes (*Hakea*) is beautiful *and* prickly. Similarly, if unwelcome street visitors are a problem you can build a fence and get a dog, or use prickly perimeter plantings.

Neighbours, Streets and Noise

Do you need to screen the house, windows or garden from neighbours, streets or noise? If so, you'll need to consider how tall the plants need to be, and how wide they can spread.

Secluded, Intimate Areas

Do you want a small, secluded spot in the garden with complete privacy where you can read a book or make love? If you do, plan for it early because the average suburban houseblock has but few spots with this potential. Plant screenings all around except for a narrow, inviting entranceway.

Screening out two-storey neighbouring buildings can be difficult. If the building is close to the boundary, you can plant tall, narrow trees (poplars and candle pines are good), but otherwise you'll need to plant a tall screen immediately around each private area. If you don't mind *shady* seclusion, choose a low tree or tall shrub with a dense canopy (e.g. *Cotoneaster*, *Viburnum tinus*). Standard Weeping Mulberries are unbeatable for summer shade (they're deciduous in winter).

Climate and Microclimate

Frosts

You can ameliorate frosts by planting trees, or choose plants that are frost-resistant.

Hot Winds

Hot winds are disastrous for many plants, especially if they're combined with scorching late-afternoon sun. Once again, you can choose hardy plants (see Drought-tolerant Plants on p. 83), or establish windbreaks so that more tender species will survive.

Other Climatic Extremes

Does your garden experience climatic extremes like very dry summers or very cold winters? If so, your design can to some extent ameliorate these effects, but your best bet will be to choose suitable plants (see Drought-tolerant Plants on p. 83).

Structures

Do you want a pergola, carport, verandah, archway, toolshed, retaining wall, steps, fence, gate? If so, you'll need to decide where it is to go, and which material—wood, stone, or metal—most suits your budget and taste.

You can design the structure to stand out and become a focal point, or you can choose more subtle colours and materials (wood and stone are particularly effective) so that the structure blends in with the surroundings. Let your own taste be your guide.

Garden Furniture

Aesthetic Additions

Would you like a sculpture, birdbath, wind chimes or Japanese water sculpture? These add sensual appeal to your garden. Visual aesthetics predominate in garden design, but remember those other senses. When buying wind chimes, close your eyes and tinkle it (no point buying a chime that looks great but sounds lousy!). Birds add song and colour, and the sound of a water sculpture or fountain is always restful.

Seating, Tables, Play Equipment

Will you build a seat/bench/chairs, table, swing? They're well worth the effort and cost if you'll spend a lot of time outside. Fixed or movable? I prefer movable furniture for its versatility: when you want a change of scene you can rearrange garden furniture in the same way as household furniture.

Water Features

Do you want a pond? Large or small? You can build a small pond almost anywhere, but you have an advantage if there's a slope on your land; for a pond to look 'natural' it should be placed at or near the lowest point.

Ponds are available preformed (expensive and almost always kidney-shaped), or you can buy even pricier liner for larger ponds, but a cheap and effective alternative is the heaviest grade of Forticon™ plastic (the black is more attractive than the orange) used to line a hole you've dug and then lined with sand.

Will there be an associated stream, waterway, waterfall, fountain or rockery? Pumps will allow you to recirculate water, but beware: they need maintenance (and so will your pond), and are expensive to buy and run.

Fish are cheaper than pumps, though you'll need to make your pond deep enough for them to escape cats (even then, there are other predators: a gardening acquaintance welcomed a crane visiting her pond until she realised, too late, the reason for its interest!).

Waterlilies look lovely, but you need a largish pond in a sunny spot for them to thrive. Choose other kinds of water plants for shady ponds.

Choice of Plants

Edible Plants

Do you want a vegetable, herb or fruit garden? Prioritise areas for food production, because vegetables and fruit need lots of sunlight (exceptions include rhubarb, celery, currants and bramble fruits, which tolerate more shade). Choose the sunniest area in your garden. If there is no sunny area and you're serious about growing vegetables, consider pruning or lopping trees to provide more sun. Expensive, but not as expensive as struggling forever with an unproductive vegetable garden. And tree roots, especially those of eucalypts, pines, willows and poplars, will rapidly invade your vegetable plot and suck the nutrients and water out of the soil.

On the other hand, many fruiting plants are ornamental and will co-exist happily in the shrubbery or garden border. Pomegranates, loquats, plums, currants, silver beets, eggplants, cherry tomatoes and tub (compact) varieties of squash will thrive amongst roses and perennials if given plenty of sun and a little extra fertiliser.

Herb Gardens

Herb gardens are best sited close to the back or front door, especially if your focus is on culinary herbs. Sunny sites intensify the flavour of most herbs.

Irrigation

Will you install a watering system? You may prefer movable sprinklers and hoses to a fixed drippers or micro-jets. Or you can choose drought-tolerant plants and minimise watering.

Maintenance

How much time will you have to maintain the garden? Certain plants, like roses, need regular pruning, fertilising and spraying (though new rose cultivars are becoming less labour-intensive and more pest-resistant all the time). Many bulbs (like tulips, hyacinths and gladioli) need to be dug up, divided, and stored before replanting the following season for the best flowers. Other plants are low-maintenance: just plant and forget (though almost all shrubs—even Australian natives— benefit from an annual light prune to keep them compact and shapely).

Overall Effects

Think about overall effects: do you prefer open space (say, a lawn bordered by garden beds), or a series of smaller garden 'rooms' leading into each other?

Scented Plants

Reserve places for scented plants (near entertaining areas or close to bedroom windows). You can choose plants with scented foliage (pelargoniums, thymes and mints) or flowers (roses, violets, jasmine, and a personal favourite, *Philadelphus*).

Vistas

Are there any views you want to preserve? Vistas you want to create (say, through a window from a favourite armchair in your

---

TIP

Essential Checklist
Consider the following to prevent any expensive design mistakes.

DO
- ensure adequate drainage around foundations
- site deciduous/evergreen plants to reduce heating/cooling costs
- consider low-maintenance plants
- consider water-saving designs

DON'T
- plant large trees close to buildings
- plant excessively vigorous climbers on structures too weak to support them

---

lounge room, or from the kitchen while you're washing up)?

Visual Aesthetics

What appeals to you aesthetically? Colourful flowers all year? And do you like to cut them for the house? Or do you prefer the more restful textural effects achieved with different *foliage* types? Some gardeners like evergreens; others choose the stunning autumn leaves and winter branches of deciduous plants.

Step 3: Draw a Rough-scale Plan of the Existing Site

If you still have building plans that show the house on the block, you can use these as a base. Otherwise, pace out or measure dimensions as accurately as possible (take as much care as you can, but don't get too paranoid—20 centimetres here or there make less difference to garden beds than they do to house plans!). Just use scrap paper and a clipboard while you're out in the garden pacing. Mark distances, structures, trees, paths, slope (with arrows) and, if necessary, houses, carports and other structures on neighbouring properties that you wish to screen. Mark the windows on your house, especially those you look out of often. Mark north.

Step 4: Draw a Working Plan of the Site

Existing Parameters
Take your rough plan inside to a well-lit table and transfer your scribbles to as large a piece of graph paper as you can find. Sketch to scale, lightly, and in HB pencil. Don't worry about dead-straight ruled lines at this stage. Have a good eraser—a *very* good eraser—at hand.

House and boundaries will probably remain unchanged from your draft plan (though you may want to add or provide space for a carport), as will large trees or other features that you're sure you want to retain.

Major Features
Now is the time to start transferring your list of needs and wants (the answers to Step 2 questions) onto the plan. Add the largish structures you'd like to include, in the places you think they'd best and most appropriately fit: chook run, garden shed, clothes line and so on. Sketch in entertaining areas, lawns, swimming pool, and garden bed areas. It's a good idea to set aside a sunny area for a vegie garden now, too, especially if sunny areas are limited by factors outside your control (e.g. large trees or

buildings on neighbouring properties). Don't worry about detail at this stage (you need to know your vegie garden will be big enough to include the range of food plants that you want, but you'll get bogged down—sorry—in detail if you try to plan precisely where the carrots and tomatoes will go at this stage).

Another option is to draw these features roughly to scale on a separate piece of paper, label them, cut them out, and jigsaw them around on your plan, as you would when planning furniture in a room (but remember that you have more flexibility, because you can change the shape of chook runs and entertaining areas more easily than that of sofas and refrigerators).

While you're playing around with options, think about those problem areas, vistas to be preserved, and neighbours to be screened. Perhaps there's an existing shady tree that's perfect for sheltering an entertaining area, or a bog that needs draining before you can pave the area. Take these problem sites into account. If you've waited and thought for long enough before sitting down and putting pencil to paper, this should happen relatively easily because you'll know your site well. Once again, don't get too hung up on plant selection, or details of what kind of paving or brand of barbecue you want. You're sorting your garden into areas that will be practical and effective—pleasing aesthetics will flow more easily from this than from a higgledy-piggledy hotchpotch.

Minor Features
Once you've decided where the major features of your garden should go, you can start playing around with specific shapes. Decide where linking paths should lead (slightly curved is visually pleasing, but make them too curved and you'll find yourself cutting off the corner unless the sightline is blocked). Decide where screening plants should go: you'll probably want to screen compost bins from the entertaining area, the swimming pool from neighbours, your bedroom window from the street and so on. You may like to

> **TIP**
>
> **Sightlines** are important in design because on level ground people tend to choose the shortest route from Point A to Point B: a straight line. Should a path deviate significantly from this line, people will ignore the path and cut the corner unless there is a visual or physical obstruction (bush, screen, pond) between points A and B.

improve access to the henhouse (where should the gate be?), and you can jigsaw the barbecue and seating in the entertaining area.

It's at this point that you can start incorporating more of the wonderful ideas you've gleaned from books and open gardens: surfaces for paths, effective screening plants, beautiful seating. Hang on to that flexibility—you might have your heart set on a rectangular picnic table you've seen in a magazine, but an oval one could fit more neatly against that curved raised bed so that the edge of the wall can double as seating.

You should still be concentrating on form and overall effect. Try to avoid incorporating too many different materials in your garden—bricks, slate, wood, metal, and stone—because too many different textures tends to give an impression of clutter.

If you like formal effects, the shapes on your plan will be straight-edged and/or symmetrical, even at this early stage of planning, and certainly well before you're up to choosing plants. For less formal effects, your plan should look *smooth*, with flowing curves and areas blending into one another, and with few sharp angles.

When you've finished, your working plan will define different areas of the garden with scrawled arrows and captions such as:

- entertaining area (BBQ here? seating here? brick paving)
- shrubbery (*note:* entertaining area— scented plants, also shrubs tall enough to screen compost bins)

- flower bed (sun lovers)
- shrubbery (shaded till late afternoon)
- lush evergreens (ferns?), tropical effect (heavy shade)
- lawn
- chook run
- side-garden (screening shrubs minimum of 3 metres to block neighbour's window)
- path (same bricks as entertaining area)
- space for swimming pool (plant with small perennials and annuals)
- full sun and hot northerlies
- keep clear, plants to 1 metre maximum to preserve view of city

and so on.

Step 5: Check and Revise the Plan So Far

Take your revised plan outside and walk around the site with it. Try to visualise how the finished garden will look. Is the entertaining area really large enough? Is that bed along the fence wide enough to support screening shrubs? Will that existing tree shade the swimming pool? Keep jotting notes and alterations to remind yourself what needs to be changed.

It's a good idea at this stage to invite a knowledgeable gardening friend along (maybe even the same one you invited to lunch before). They'll contribute practical advice as to whether your plans are workable, and may point out problems you've overlooked. You can also ask about suitable plants, explaining the effect you're after. They should be able to tell you whether the plants will grow or, if not, why not.

Step 6: Add the Final Details

Large Trees, Shrubs and Hedges
At last you're up to choosing plants and getting quotes on paving materials. Starting with the largest plants (trees, tall or wide shrubs, screening specimens), mark them onto your plan as circles. The diameter of each

circle should be scaled to the mature diameter of the plant. This is essential: it's very easy to overplant a new area, because even the most experienced gardeners find it difficult to envisage a tiny seedling as a mature tree. Overplanting is a terrible waste of money because your garden will be hopelessly over-crowded, with plants failing to thrive due to competition unless you rip out the excess specimens. On the other hand, you might deliberately allow for a degree of overlap when planning hedging or screening effects.

If you have enough plant knowledge, you'll be able to identify the plants by name at this stage, but don't worry if you can't. It's okay to note the specimen as 'evergreen tree, 5 metres × 4 metres spread'. If it's beside the entertaining area, you may want scented leaves or flowers, or you may want the flowers to complement a particular colour scheme. Ask your gardening friends or staff at a plant nursery which trees meet these criteria.

When choosing large, slow-growing or long-lived specimens that are difficult and expensive to remove if you make a mistake, it's best to see a mature specimen, either in a botanic or private garden, or in a book, before you make the final decision. Many plant nurseries keep books that illustrate the trees and plants they sell, but beware—the lush, healthy bush illustrated thriving in ideal growing conditions often bears little resemblance to the straggly, sparse and diseased specimen struggling in your suburb. Ask the nursery assistant what conditions the plant needs to thrive.

Alternatively, visit botanic and open gardens and look for plants that meet your criteria (park staff and garden owners will identify their trees for you).

Surfaces and Structural Materials

You should also be deciding on surface and structural materials now. Get quotes (cheap sources are listed in Chapter 5), estimate overall costs, and revise your initial choice if price is prohibitive. Alternatively, you may decide your budget won't stretch to paving just yet, and that's fine too. Instead, leave the area bare if you think you'll be paving in six months time, plant annuals if you'll pave in one or two years time, and groundcovers (easy to remove) if you won't be able to afford paving for five years or so.

Of course, you may well change your mind by then ... but that's the beauty of gardening. If you've planned in this way, leaving your options open, you won't need to spend thousands of dollars removing established trees or hiring jackhammers to break up concrete.

Small Plants and Groundcovers

When you've chosen the larger plants and surfaces, you can begin filling in the smaller shrubs, climbers and groundcovers. Once again, start with larger and move down to smaller. Medium-sized shrubs and ground-covers should be marked in their mature diameter; you can fill in with perennials, annuals or small shrubs. You're still working on paper, and even at this stage of planning it's merely a matter of using the eraser to make changes. That's the beauty of planning in this way, whether you're adapting an established garden or creating a new one.

Remember the basics of good garden design: resist the temptation, if you can, of collecting one of each plant—mass or repeat plantings really do give a professional and uni-fying feel to a garden. Of course, every keen gardener, including me, succumbs to impulse buying. That's fine if you're adding these plants to an existing well-structured garden, but it's disastrous if your whole plan is based on impulse purchases. Such a garden will look 'bitty', uncoordinated, and lack cohesion and structure ... you have been warned!

Step 7: Implementing the Plan

The method you choose to implement your plan will depend on your expertise, time, enthusiasm and budget, though I suspect that

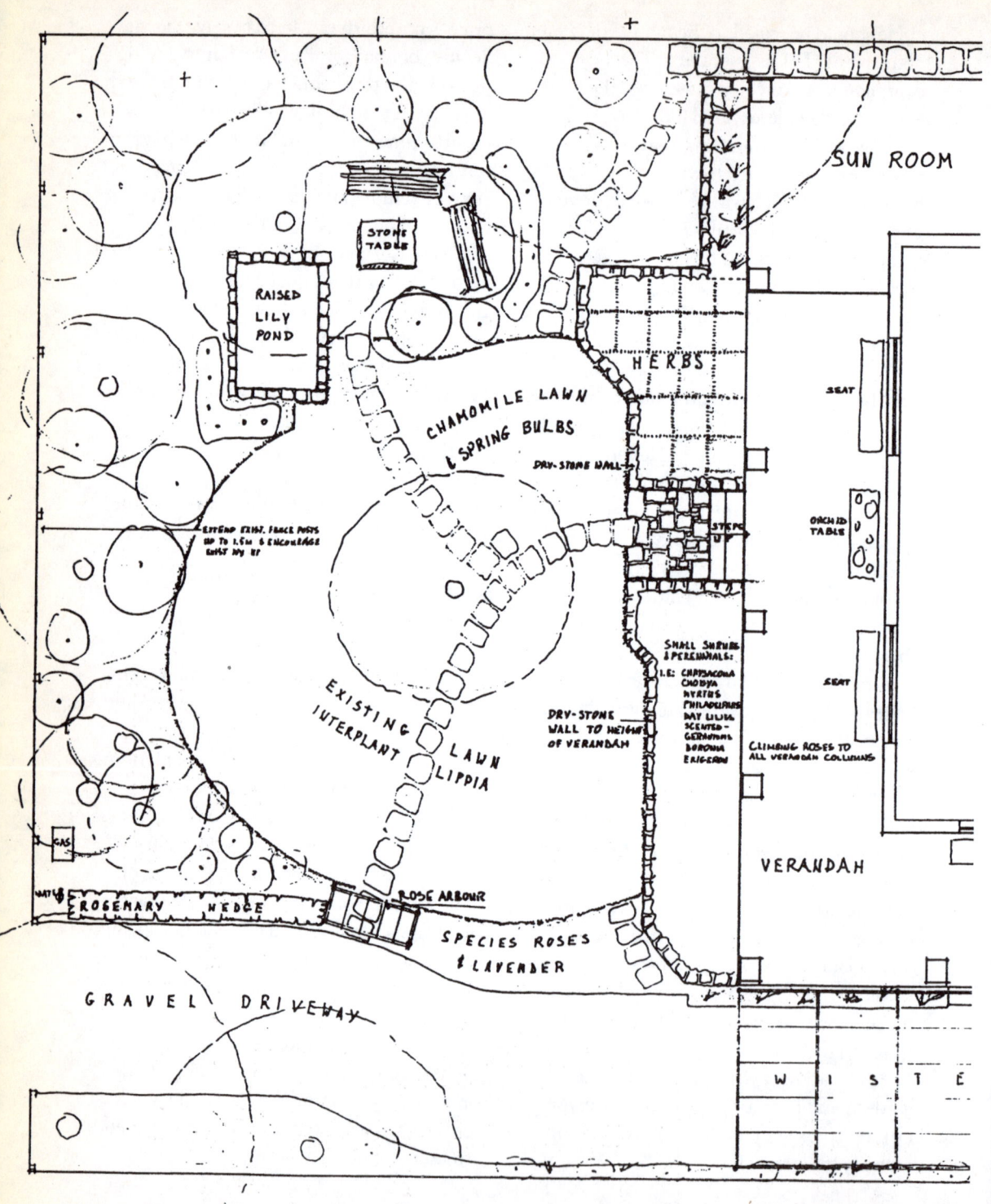

SUN ROOM

STONE TABLE

RAISED LILY POND

CHAMOMILE LAWN & SPRING BULBS

HERBS

SEAT

DRY-STONE WALL

ORCHID TABLE

EXTEND EXIST. FENCE POSTS UP TO 1.8M & ENCOURAGE CLIMB. IVY UP

EXISTING LAWN INTERPLANT LIPPIA

STEPS UP

SMALL SHRUBS & PERENNIALS: I.E: CHOISYA CHOISYA MYRTUS PHILADELPHUS DAY LILY SCENTED- GERANIUM BORONIA ERIGERON

DRY-STONE WALL TO HEIGHT OF VERANDAH

SEAT

CLIMBING ROSES TO ALL VERANDAH COLUMNS

VERANDAH

WATER

ROSEMARY HEDGE

GAS

ROSE ARBOUR

SPECIES ROSES & LAVENDER

GRAVEL DRIVEWAY

WISTE

Garden plans vary in price and degree of detail but should be to scale. These sections are of 'concept plans' drawn by a landscape contractor. They provide more than enough information for clients to visualise the finished garden. Although not visible here, the plan also includes scale and aspects (north).

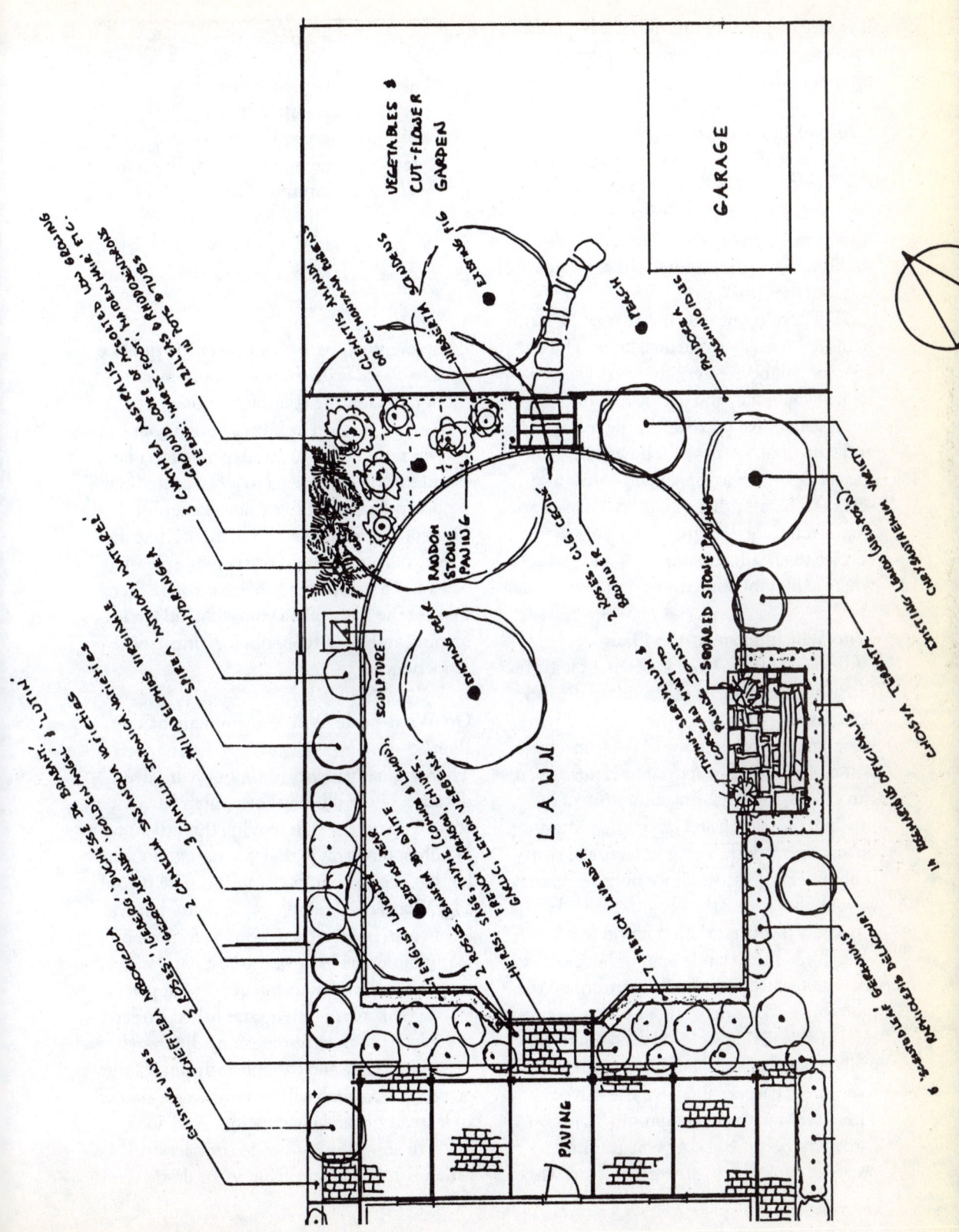

VEGETABLES & CUT-FLOWER GARDEN

GARAGE

CLEMATIS ARMANDII OR CL. MONTANA RUBENS

WISTERIA SINENSIS

ESPALIER FIG

PEACH

PLANTING SLIDERS

3 CAMELLIA AUSTRALIS ASSOCIATED WITH MARDAM RHODODENDRONS

3 GROUND COVER-FOOT AZALEAS

FERNS: HYDRANGEA

ANTHURIUM MILLARBELLA STEEL

3 CAMELLIA SASANQUA VARIETIES

RANDOM STONE PAVING

SCULPTURE

SEGMENTED STONE PAVING

2 CAMELLIA VARIETIES 'GARGE', GOLDEN VARIETIES

CHOISYA TERNATA

EXISTING LEMON

CHRYSANTHEMUM VARIETY

DUCHESSE DE BRABANT

2 CAMELLIA SASANQUA VARIETIES

L A W N

BUTLERS OAK

ENGLISH LAVENDER

TRUNKS SEGMENTED CAPTAIN WARF SPACE

CL BANKS 3 MONTHLIES

HERBS: SAGE, THYME (COMMON, LEMON), FRESH TARRAGON, VERBENA GARLIC, LEMON, CHIVES

2 ROSES: SILVER 'DELIGHTE', LEMON

7 FRENCH LAVENDER

PAVING

2 ROSES: CL GECILE BRONNER

SCHEFFLERA ARBORICOLA 'DUCHESSE DE BRABANT'

EXISTING NATIVE FLOSS 5 ROSES

NICOTIANA & LILIUM

RAPHIOLEPIS INDICA & GERANIUMS

RAPHIOLEPIS DELICATA

11 GARDENIA STANDARDS

if you've had the commitment to design your own garden you'll be keen to implement the plan as well.

Order of Implementation

Think carefully about in which order to develop the garden. Which areas are most urgent and important? Utility areas are usually more urgent than recreation areas: I find it easy to do without a barbecue area, but not a clothes line.

Will developing one area first make it difficult to access a second area later? The answers will be different for every garden: look at your plan, and decide for yourself.

It's generally best to do all the major earth and structural work first, followed by plantings of slow-growing specimens, trees and screens. You may then prefer to *complete* one small section of the garden at a time so you can see the results of your work and feel you're achieving something.

Who Will Implement the Plan?

Will you do all the work yourself, or will you hire a mini-bobcat for the major earthworks? Bobcats aren't cheap to hire (usually by the hour or half-day), but one of these machines will move as much soil in a few hours as you can in weeks of back-breaking work of picking, shovelling and barrowing. Many bobcat operators have a good sense of contours and may discuss minor improvements to your plan before they begin the work, especially if you ask their opinion first.

Will you hire a landscaper or builder to construct walls, pergolas, carports, or do the job yourself? This depends, of course, on your expertise: we built our own sleeper retaining walls and stone walls, but hired contractors to erect our carport and pave the driveway. These decisions are a compromise for most gardeners, because budget constraints prevent us from hiring the contractors who

> ### TIP
> - Laying down a garden hose to outline the shape of a garden bed will promote smooth curves.
> - Steps are generally better shallow and wide than narrow and steep.
> - Retaining walls need a certain batter and base width for stability.

complete the job in a fraction of the time we take to do so. Still, there is enormous satisfaction in creating your own garden.

And should you decide to design your own garden rather than hiring experts, don't be daunted: you don't need to be an accredited landscape architect to achieve beautiful results (remember that kitchen!). There are plenty of tricks to help you achieve pleasing lines and forms in the garden; if you're doing most of the hard yakka yourself, read landscaping and 'how-to' books for hints (see Appendix 1).

On What Scale Will You Implement the Plan?

There's usually plenty of time—years, even decades. Use it all. Better to wait a few years to save up for the right paving than to immediately spread gravel that you hate to look at but later can't bear to replace because it cost a bit. Plans need not be implemented in one fell swoop. In fact, the *process* is, for me and many gardeners I know, the best part. Why else do keen gardeners forever rip out perfectly good areas of their established gardens to replace them with something different?

So be flexible and patient: at the end of the process your garden will be a true expression of your creativity and imagination. And don't forget to enjoy the journey to completion, which is, to me, as satisfying as the destination.

Conclusion

This book is a starting point. Once you've begun to investigate money-smart ways of gardening, you'll be surprised at the new opportunities that arise for you. Saving money in gardening, as in all areas of life, is often merely a matter of looking with unpeeled eyes beyond the first obvious choice to where the unexpected alternatives reside. Grab them when you can.

As you explore opportunities, you'll build up a network of friends and knowledgeable gardeners who can help you in developing your skills. Go to markets, nurseries, garden expos, garage and trash-and-treasure sales, even if you don't have the money to buy at that particular time. In the process, you'll learn where to go for bargains and—even better—how to recognise them when you see them. Share your knowledge freely with anyone you think might benefit.

Join garden clubs, watch TV gardening programs, visit open gardens, read books and magazines, visit and revisit your local botanic garden, chat to gardeners over the front fence as you walk down your street. You'll soak up garden lore without having to do any boring rote work; after six months or a year you'll suddenly realise you're viewing plants and gardens in an entirely different way. It's an exciting, intuitive moment, like suddenly

understanding a mathematical concept: a moment to treasure. You've enriched yourself in a way that cannot—and should not—be measured in dollars.

The world of gardening is a vast one, big enough to accommodate any taste. Of course, some options are so expensive that they'll always be unavailable to the impecunious gardener, no matter what money-saving techniques are employed—but then, do you really *need* Italian marble fountains, original sculptures and rare newly imported plant varieties to enjoy your garden? Make, instead, a Japanese bamboo water spout, join a sculpture class and create your own originals, propagate special plants yourself. Bigger and dearer is not *better* when it comes to gardens, merely *different*. You don't need to scale down your expectations, but only to glance sideways. Gardens may be large, small, formal, informal, flowery, textural, influenced by other gardens in every continent and culture of the world ... or by none. The choice is entirely yours.

It's also up to you, of course, but living as harmoniously as you can in the environment is money-smart too. Not necessarily for you, personally, in the short term—still, you'll gain in the long term, as will future generations. And we're talking smart in ways that are more important than money—how can we put a price on the health of our environment, on the happiness of future generations, on damage to immune systems, on biodiversity, or on pest resistance to chemicals? Economists try, but I think some things are just too big to measure this way. How many dollars to look out of your kitchen window to see the beautiful garden that you designed? To smell the flowers you raised yourself from seed? To spend an hour planting seedlings in rich, healthy garden soil?

So although this book is about saving money in your garden, the end—for you, as a reader—is in the garden itself and your enjoyment of it. Saving money is only the means. Hunt out bargains, haggle, cut corners, look for alternatives, but don't forget your reason for doing so. Enjoy your garden.

Appendices

Appendix 1: Further Reading (Books and Magazines)

General

Lloyd, C. (1983), *The Adventurous Gardener*, Penguin Books, London.

Lloyd, C. (1985), *The Well-Tempered Garden*, Penguin Books, London.

Page, R. (1995), *The Education of a Gardener*, The Harvill Press, London.

Wright, M. (1978), *Complete Book of Gardening*, Penguin Books, London.

Yates Garden Guide Centennial Edition 1895–1995 (1997), HarperCollins, Australia.

Plants and Plant Selection

Beckett, K. (1985), *The Concise Encyclopaedia of Garden Plants*, Orbis Publishing, London.

Craig, C. (ed.) (1997), *500 Popular Garden Plants for Australian Gardeners*, Random House, Milson's Point, Australia.

French, J. (1995), *Plants That Never Say Die*, Lothian Books, Port Melbourne, Australia.

Macoboy, S. (1986), *What Flower Is That?*, Landsdowne Publishing, Sydney, Australia.

Macoboy, S. (1989), *What Shrub Is That?*, Landsdowne Publishing, Sydney Australia.

Macoboy, S. (1996), *What Tree Is That?*, Landsdowne Publishing, Sydney, Australia.

Macoboy, S., Rodd. T. & Spurway M. (eds) (1991), *The Reader's Digest Gardeners' Encyclopaedia of Plants and Flowers*, Reader's Digest Pty Ltd, Surrey Hills, Australia.

Phillips, R. & Foy, N. (1990), *Herbs*, Pan Books, London.

Phillips, R. & Rix, M. (1989), *Bulbs*, Pan Books, London.

—— (1989), *Shrubs*, Pan Books, London.

—— (1991), *Perennials*, vols 1 & 2, Pan Books, London.

Botany and Taxonomy

Capon, B. (1990), *Botany for Gardeners: An Introduction and Guide*, Timber Press, Portland, Oregon.

Propagation

Gardiner, A. (1988), *Modern Plant Propagation*, Lothian Books, Port Melbourne, Australia.

Kelly, J. (1996), *Growing Plants from Seed*, Ward Lock, London.

Klock, P. (1997), *Plant Propagation: Seeds, Cuttings, Division, Layering, Grafting*, Ward Lock, London.

Plumridge, J. (1976), *How to Propagate Plants*, Lothian Books, Port Melbourne, Australia.

Landscaping Materials (composting, mulching, fertilisers, soils)

Clayton, S. (1993), *The Reverse Garbage Garden*, Hyland House, South Melbourne, Australia.

Clayton, S. (1994), *The Reverse Garbage Mulch Book*, Hyland House, South Melbourne, Australia.

Hendreck, K. (1977), *Soils*, CSIRO Division of Soils, Melbourne, Australia.

—— 1978), *Composting*, CSIRO Division of Soils, Melbourne, Australia.

—— (1978), *Food for Plants*, CSIRO Division of Soils, Melbourne, Australia.

—— (1978), *What's Wrong with My Soil?*, CSIRO Division of Soils, Melbourne, Australia.

—— (1979), *Organic Matter and Soils*, CSIRO Division of Soils, Melbourne, Australia.

Pest Control

Carson, R. (1962), *Silent Spring*, Penguin Books, Middlesex, UK.

French, J. (1990), *Natural Control of Garden Pests*, Aird Books, Flemington, Victoria.

Jones, D. & Elliot, R. (1986), *Pests, Diseases and Ailments of Australian Plants*, Lothian Books, Melbourne, Australia.

McMaugh, J. (1985), *What Garden Pest or Disease Is That?*, Lansdowne Press, New South Wales, Australia.

Short, K. (1994), *Quick Poison Slow Poison: Pesticide Risk in the Lucky Country*, Kate Short, Wollombi Rd, St Albans, NSW.

Victorian Department of Food and Agriculture, (1992), *Pest Control in Home Gardens*, Victorian Department of Food and Agriculture Gardens Advisory Service.

Woodward, P (1997), *Pest-Repellent Plants*, Hyland House, South Melbourne, Australia.

Design and Planning

Brookes, J. (1991), *Your Garden Design Book*, Lothian Books, Port Melbourne, Australia.

Hobhouse, P. (1997), *Penelope Hobhouse's Garden Designs*, Hodder Headline, Australia.

Patrick, J. (1989), *Australian Garden Designs*, Viking O'Neil (Penguin Books), Ringwood, Australia.

Trapp, S. J. von (1997), *Landscaping from the Ground Up*, Taunton Books, Connecticut, USA.

Saving on Water

Hartshorne, H. (1995), *Plants for Dry Gardens*, Allen & Unwin, St Leonards, NSW, Australia.

Hendreck, K. (1979), *When Should I Water?*, CSIRO Division of Soils, Melbourne, and Rellim Technical Publications, Adelaide, Australia.

Nottle, T. (1996), *Gardens of the Sun*, Kangaroo Press, Kenthurst, NSW, Australia.

Patrick, J. (1994), *Beautiful Gardens with Less Water*, Lothian Books, Port Melbourne, Australia.

Walsh, K. (1995), *Water Saving Gardening*, Reed Books, Australia.

Magazines

The following are the result of a brief perusal of the shelves of my three local newsagencies. The magazines are available at time of writing, but be aware that new ventures come and go, and that availability may vary with location.

Australian Horticulture
Australian House and Garden
The Australian Gardener
BBC Gardeners' World (UK)
Country Gardener
Earth Garden
Gardening Australia
Gardens Illustrated (UK)
Grass Roots
Landscaping Australian Style
Permaculture International Journal
Practical Hydroponics and Greenhouses
Warm Earth
Your Garden

Earth Garden, Grass Roots, Permaculture International and *Warm Earth* contain many handy money-saving tips.

Appendix 2: Educational Organisations

Adult education programs offer a variety of courses which change from term to term and year to year.

Tasmania

Institute of Natural Resources (Hobart, Burnie and Launceston campuses)
PO Box 1234
Burnie Tas. 7320
Tel. 03 6233 7424
Certificate and diploma courses in horticulture. Single modules may be taken space permitting.

Institute of Adult Education and Community Services
51 York St
Launceston Tas. 7250
Tel. 03 6336 2802
Short hobby courses (e.g. birdscaping, bonsai, cottage gardening, landscaping).

Queensland

Brisbane Institute of TAFE (Grovely Campus)
Fitzsimmons St
Grovely Qld 4053
Tel. 07 3354 5506
Certificate and diploma courses in horticulture. Allow enrolments in individual modules space permitting.

There are also regional country TAFES and campuses (not listed here).

Adult Education, Itheco Campus
Locked Bag 10
Kelvin Grove
DC Qld 4059
Tel. 07 3259 9111
Short hobby courses (e.g. permaculture, herbs).

Western Australia

South Metropolitan College of TAFE (Murdoch, Midland & Rockingham campuses)
Murdoch Drive
Murdoch WA 6150
Tel: 08 9310 0444
Offer certificate and diploma courses. Allow enrolment in individual modules, space permitting. There are also regional TAFES and campuses (not listed here).

WA Training Information Centre
Ground Floor, Albert Facey House
469 Wellington St
Perth WA 6000
Freecall 1800 999 167; local 08 9325 9322
Adult education programs: short hobby courses (e.g. design, herbs, fruit, small gardens, bonsai, scented plants, permaculture) offered through TAFE Centres.

Australian Capital Territory

Canberra Institute of Technology
PO Box 826
Canberra ACT 2601
Tel. 02 6207 3100
Offer certificate and diploma courses in horticulture (nursery, landscape, parks). Allow enrolments in individual modules, space permitting. Also offer adult education short hobby courses (e.g. herbs, plant propagation, design theory, permaculture).

New South Wales

Northern Sydney Institute of TAFE, Ryde (Horticulture Section)
20 Blaxland Rd
Ryde NSW 2112
Tel. 02 9448 6222
Diploma and certificate courses in horticulture. Allow enrolment in individual modules, space permitting. Horticulture also offered at Pastow and Richmond TAFES, plus regional country centres (Charlestown, Orange).

WEA (Adult Education)
72 Bathurst St
Sydney NSW 2000
Tel. 02 9264 2781
Occasionally offer gardening courses (e.g. garden design, landscaping your garden).

South Australia

WEA (Adult Education)
223 Angas St
Adelaide SA 5000
Tel. 08 8223 1979
Offer short courses (e.g. plant propagation, cottage gardening, landscaping, herbs, practical home gardening, rose gardens).

Torrens Valley Institute of TAFE
(Brookway Park Campus)
State Horticulture Centre
Brookway Drive
Campbelltown SA 5074
Tel. 08 8207 8791
Certificates and diplomas in horticulture (e.g. turf, nursery, amenity, landscaping). Allow enrolments in individual modules, space permitting. Campuses also exist at O'Halloran, Mt Barker and Gawler.

Victoria

Institute of Land and Food Resources
University of Melbourne
Parkville, Vic. 3052
Freecall 1800 815 803; local 03 9344 0276
Offer certificate and diploma courses in horticulture.

Council of Adult Education
256 Flinders St
Melbourne Vic. 3000
Tel. 03 9652 0611
Offer short hobby courses (e.g. design, courtyard design, bonsai, birds in the garden).

Northern Territory

NT University
Darwin NT 0909
Freecall 1800 061 963; local 08 8946 6666
Offer certificate and diploma courses in horticulture.

Centralian College
PO Box 795
Alice Springs NT 0871
Tel. 08 8959 5400
Offer courses in horticulture.

Appendix 3:
Botanic Gardens

Most identify plants; some charge a fee for this service so check with your local nursery first.

Darwin Botanic Gardens and NT Herbarium
Palmerston NT 0831
Tel. 08 8999 4516
Refer home gardens enquiries to Department of Primary Industries. Plant identification service.

Royal Botanic Gardens Sydney
Mrs Macquarie Rd
Sydney NSW 2000
Tel. 02 9231 8111
No advisory service, but identify plants.

Australian National Botanic Gardens
PO Box 1777
Canberra ACT 2601
Tel. 02 6250 9450
Plant identification service for Australian native species. Answer queries about Australian native plants (culture etc.) on an unofficial basis.

Royal Botanic Gardens Melbourne
Birdwood Ave
South Yarra Vic. 3141
Tel. 03 9252 2300
Refer queries to College of Horticulture. Identify plants (fee applies).

Brisbane Botanic Gardens
Mt Coot-tha Rd
Toowong Qld 4066
Tel. 07 3403 2536
Answer home garden queries on an unofficial basis. Identify plants (service free at time of writing).

Botanic Gardens of Adelaide
North Ter.
Adelaide SA 5000
Tel. 08 8228 2322
No home gardens advisory service but run Plant Clinic Days twice monthly. Plant identification service.

Kings Park and Botanic Garden
Fraser Ave
West Perth WA 6005
Tel. 08 9480 3600
Plant identification service. Master gardeners there trained to staff a gardens advisory service.

Royal Tasmanian Botanical Gardens
Queens Domain
Hobart Tas. 7000
Tel. 03 6234 6299
Plant identification service. No official advisory service but answer garden queries on an ad hoc basis.

For a detailed listing of all Australian Botanic Gardens, see Murray Fagg and Jan Wilson's book *Directory of Australian Botanic Gardens and Arboretums* (Australian National Botanic Gardens, Canberra), available from the Australian National Botanic Gardens bookshop.

Appendix 4:
Government Organisations

National Registration Authority for Agricultural and Veterinary Chemicals
Level 1/10 National Court
Barton ACT 2600
or
PO Box E240
Kingston ACT 2604
Tel. 02 6272 5158

Tasmanian Department of Primary Industries, Water and Environment
PO Box 44A
Hobart Tas. 7001
Tel. 02 6233 8011

South Australian Department of Primary Industries and Resources
Grenfell Centre
25 Grenfell St
or
PO Box 1671
Adelaide SA 5001
General enquiries tel. 08 8226 0222

Western Australian Department of Primary Industries
3 Baron-Hay Ct
South Perth WA 6151
Garden Advisory Centre general garden enquiries tel. 1902292555; subscriber enquiries tel. 08 9474 3008

Western Australian Health Department
Environmental Health (Pesticide Safety)
1A Brockway Rd
Mt Claremont WA 6010
or
PO Box 8172
Stirling St
Perth WA 6849
Tel. 08 9383 4244

Victorian Department of Natural Resources and Environment
8 Nicholson St
or
PO Box 500
East Melbourne Vic. 3002
General enquiries tel. 03 9637 8000

Queensland Department of Primary Industries
Primary Industries Building
80 Ann St
or

PO Box 46
Brisbane Qld 4001
Home gardens tel. 07 3239 3116

New South Wales Department of Agriculture
161 Kite St
or
Locked Bag 21
Orange NSW 2800
Tel. 02 6391 3100

Northern Territory Department of Primary Industry and Fisheries
Berrimah Agricultural Research Centre
(Berrimah Farm)
PO Box 990
Darwin NT 0801
Tel. 08 8999 5511

Appendix 5: Garden Clubs and Plant Societies

Societies that specialise in the following plant groups meet in capital cities and regional centres around Australia. Check the *Yellow Pages* and *White Pages* for details.

African violets
Australian plants
Begonias
Bonsai
Cacti and succulents
Camellias/azaleas/rhododendrons
Cottage-garden plants
Carnivorous plants
Daffodils
Day lilies
Ferns
Fuchsias
Gerberas
Giant pumpkin and vegetables
Herbs
Hibiscus
Irises

Liliums
Native orchids
Orchids
Pelargoniums and/or geraniums
Palms and cycads
Proteas
Rare fruits
Rare plants
Roses
Salvias

Societies also exist to support organic, permaculture, biodynamic and hydroponic gardening (look in the *Yellow Pages* and *White Pages*).

Appendix 6: Pesticides

These pesticides are a selection of those sold by my local hardware store and garden centre at time of writing. It's well worth checking value for money before spending. Where competing brands were available for similar or identical products, I calculated price, volume and active ingredient to give dearest and cheapest cost per gram. Some of the biggest differences were between ready-to-use sprays (pre-mixed in pump-packs or aerosol cans) versus ones you dilute yourself: you pay an awful lot for convenience.

I've also listed a range of organic products available—check your own local store for more.

* Denotes organic pesticides

Herbicides

GLYPHOSATE
Comkil (1 L)   100 g/L glyphosate
Davison Glyphosate 360 (1 L)
                  360 g/L glyphosate
Monsanto Roundup (1 L)
                  360 g/L glyphosate
No Grow Weedspray 450 (1 L)
                  450 g/L glyphosate

No Grow Weedspray (200 mL)
                  100 g/L glyphosate
No Grow Weedspray (250 mL)
                  450 g/L glyphosate
Zero Ready-to-use spray (750 mL)
                  3.6 g/L glyphosate
(cost of glyphosate ranged from 8c per gram to $2.70 per gram)

* Bio Speed-Weed (3 litres)
                  24 g/L fatty acids

Miticides
Kelthane Red Spider (200 mL)
                  75 g/L dicofol

Insecticides
Chemspray Rogor Aerosol (350 g)
                  0.3 g/kg dimethoate
Yates Rogor Insecticide (100 mL)
                  300 g/L dimethoate
(cost of dimethoate ranged from 30c per gram to $82.86 per gram)

Agchem Malathion (200 mL)
                  500 g/L maldison
                  44 g/L liquid hydrocarbons
Hortico Malascale (200 mL)
                  100 g/L maldison
                  480 g/L petroleum oil
(cost of maldison ranged from 9c per gram to 47c per gram)

*Agchem White Spray oil (250 mL)
                  550 g/L petroleum oil
*Ampol Pest Oil (500 mL)
                  839 g/L petroleum oil
*CRG Superior White Oil (500 mL)
                  820 g/L petroleum oil
(cost of petroleum oil ranged from 3c per gram to 8c per gram)

Lebaycid Insect Spray (100 mL)
                  550 g/L fenthion

Nemacur nematicide (300 g)
        50 g/kg fenamiphos
*Tahara Eucalyptus (500 mL)
        10 g/L eucalyptus oil
*Yates Dipel (400 g)
        4320 I.U./mg *Bacillus
        thurigiensis* var. *kurstaki*
*Hortico Derris Dust (500 g)
        7.5 g/kg rotenone
*Zest multipurpose dust (375 g)
        7.5 g/kg rotenone
        400 g/kg sulphur
        (fungicide)

PYRETHRUM SPRAYS

The active ingredients in pyrethrum sprays are pyrethrins (py) and piperonyl butoxide (pb).

Piperonyl butoxide is a synergist, essential to the effectiveness of pyrethrins (a consistent ratio in all products—approximately pb:py 4:1). The cost per gram is calculated on pyrethrins.

*AgChem Garden Safety Spray (200 mL)
        4 g/L py, 16 g/L pb
*Garden King Safety Spray (200 mL)
        4g/L py, 16 g/L pb
*Multicrop Value Pak (750 mL x 2)
        0.3 g/L py, 1.2 g/L pb
*Nurserymans Brand Pyrethrum (250 mL)
        3 g/L py, 12 g/L pb
*Pest-away Organics (500 mL)
        0.12g/L py, 0.415 g/L pb
*Timed-release Insect Spray (750 mL)
        0.3g/L py, 1.2 g/L pb
*Yates Bug Gun (750 mL)
        0.3 g/L py, 1.2 g/L pb
*Yates Green Earth Spray (750 mL)
        0.3 g/L py, 1.2 g/L pb
*Yates Slay-afe Aerosol (400 g)
        25 g/kg py,1 g/kg pb
(cost of pyrethrin ranged from 80c per gram to $125.83 per gram)

Fungicides

There are many fungicides available, often specific to particular diseases. They include Daconil, Triforene, *Bordeaux mix (copper oxychloride), and *sulphur (dustable and wetting).

Appendix 7: Fertilisers

This is a selection of fertilisers at my local garden centre (at time of writing) to give you an idea of the range available and their NPK ratios. Check dilution rates to ascertain value for money, check 'fm' (fine materials) content, and note the difference in concentrations between organic and chemical fertilisers.

* Denotes organic fertiliser

Slow Release Granules

Green Jacket Flower and Shrub 16.2-4.3-15
Green Jacket Fruit & Vegetable 20.5-4.3-10
Nutricote Outdoor Garden & Shrub
   13.3-5.8-9.7
Osmocote Australian Natives 17-1.6-8.7
Osmocote Indoor, Courtyard & Balcony
   18-4.8-9.1
Osmocote Outdoor, Tree & Shrub 18-4.8-8.3

Foliar Fertilisers

Aquasol 23-4-18
Manutec Bloom Booster 6.2-14.6-16.8
*Maxicrop Fish Emulsion 4.6-1.2-3.1
Miracle-Gro 15-13.1-12.4
Phostrogen Acid Plant Food 15-4.4-12.5
Phostrogen Plant Food 14-4.4-22.5
Phostrogen Rose Food 9-4.4-20.8
Phostrogen Tomato Food 12.5-2.2-20.3
Thrive All-purpose 27-5.5-9
Thrive Flower & Fruit 15-4-26

Balanced Fertilisers

*Dynamic Lifter 3-2.4-1.5
*Fertico All-purpose Organic Fertiliser
    2.5-3.5-2
*Galloping Garden Organic Fertiliser Pellets
    4-3-1.4
Gro-Plus Bulb Food 4.1-4.8-5.7
Gro-Plus Citrus Food 10.5-2.3-8.3
*Neutrog Blood & Bone 5-5-0
*Neutrog Organic Fertiliser 3-3.7-0
Nurseryman's Fruit & Citrus Fertiliser
    9.5-1.9-8.5
*Rapid Raiser 5-3-3
Top Complete Mineral Mix 10.5-1.8-5
*Zoo Poo (no analysis)

Specific Chemical Fertilisers

Sulphate of ammonia 21% weight/volume
Sulphate of potash 41.5% weight/weight
Urea 46%N weight/volume

Appendix 8:
Independent Living Centres

Parkinson St
Weston ACT 2611
Tel. 02 6205 1900
Fax 02 6205 1906

600 Victoria Rd
Ryde NSW 2112
PO Box 3163
Putney NSW 2112
Tel. 02 9808 2233
Fax 02 9809 7132

Cnr Goring and Cavendish Rd
Coorparoo Qld 4151
Tel. 07 3397 1224
Fax 07 3394 1013

46 Canning St
Launceston Tas. 7250
Tel. 03 6334 5899
Fax 03 6334 0045

705 Geelong Rd
Brooklyn Vic. 3025
Tel. 03 9362 6111
Fax 03 9314 9825

3 Lemnos St
Shenton Park WA 6008
Tel. 089 382 2011
Fax 089 382 2896

11 Blacks Rd
Gilles Plains SA 5086
Tel. 08 8266 5260
Fax 08 8266 5263
Freecall 1800 800 523

Pest-Repellent Plants
PENNY WOODWARD

This volume in **Australia's Best Garden Guides** contains the most useful pest-repellent plants for your garden, and includes recipes for sprays, oils and dusting powders you can make at home to organically control more than 60 common garden pests.

Penny Woodward is the author of *Penny Woodward's Australian Herbal* and *Garlic and Friends*. She has written for several gardening magazines, including *Your Garden* and the *Australian Garden Journal*.

ISBN 1 86447 028 3 $16.95 rrp

Another HYLAND HOUSE publication
available from good bookshops everywhere

The Reverse Garbage Mulch Book

SANDRA CLAYTON

Magnificent, magical, miraculous and mellow mulch. Is there anything it can't do for the garden?

The Reverse Garbage Mulch Book enables the gardener to use mulch with confidence, secure in the knowledge that the plants are receiving all the nutrition they need without the necessity for harsh chemicals. It will become a 'bible' for all organic gardeners whatever methods they use.

ISBN 1 875657 40 1 $19.95 rrp

Another HYLAND HOUSE publication

available from good bookshops everywhere

Earthworms in Australia

A comprehensive guide for gardeners, farmers, conservationists and aspiring worm farmers

DAVID MURPHY

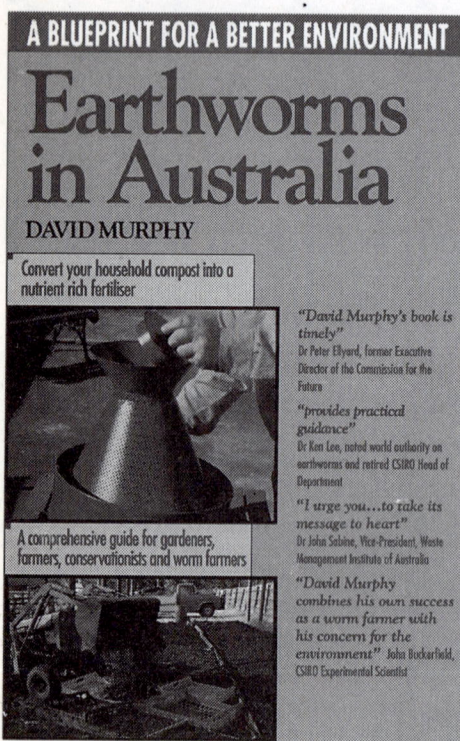

Worms convert your household compost heap into a constant supply of nutrient-rich vermicast for your garden.

'David Murphy combines his own success as a worm farmer with his concern for the environment'

(JOHN BUCKERFIELD, CSIRO EXPERIMENTAL SCIENTIST)

ISBN 1 875657 09 6 $16.95 rrp

Another HYLAND HOUSE publication

available from good bookshops everywhere